ACOUSTIC
GUITAR
PRIVATE LESSONS

THE WAY MUSIC WORKS

Understanding Notation and Building Scales, Chords, and Progressions on Guitar

By Gretchen Menn

string
letter
media

Publisher: David A. Lusterman
Editor: Adam Perlmutter
Managing Editor: Kevin Owens
Music Proofreader: Mark Althans
Design and Production: Bill Evans
Production Manager: Hugh O'Connor

Cover Photograph: Bill Evans

© 2019 String Letter Publishing, Inc.

ISBN 978-1-936604-39-5

Printed in the United States of America
All rights reserved.
This book was produced by String Letter Publishing, Inc.
941 Marina Way S., Suite E, Richmond, CA 94804
(510) 215-0010; stringletter.com

Contents

Video downloads to accompany each of the lessons and musical examples in this book are available for free at **store.acousticguitar.com/TWMW**. Just add the video tracks to your shopping cart and check out to get your free download.

Introduction

Many guitar players have an unreasonable aversion to anything that even smells like music theory. Misconceptions and excuses abound: It's too confusing. It's creatively stifling. It's all rules, and art is about breaking the rules. Such beliefs are ultimately self-defeating and unfounded. Theory is not proscriptive, but rather descriptive. It doesn't tell you what you should or should not do; it investigates, outlines, and interprets what musicians have done and how music works. Art precedes analysis.

I can't name a single accomplished musician who has studied theory and regrets it. A full view of the advantages may be elusive at the onset, and we can only truly appreciate the rewards of having a skill once we've gone to the trouble of attaining it. While great music can certainly be created without knowledge of traditional music theory—many legendary artists have come up with their own systems and nonstandard ways of relating to music. But here's my point: Your brain will conceptualize music in *some* way. Why not have it be in the way that allows you to communicate most freely with other musicians? It will stifle your creativity only as much as being literate in your native language has impeded your ability to express your thoughts, ideas, and feelings.

So familiarize yourself with music theory because it will benefit you.

Many musicians suffer artistically and professionally by attempting to insulate themselves from music theory. The coping mechanisms they concoct require far more effort with less consistent results than simply following what hundreds of years of music education has determined to be a clear and comprehensible way to present the material. Sure, you can invent your own language, but how helpful is it for communicating if you're the only one who speaks it?

As with the study of language, you don't have to dive into the esoteric to reap the benefits of the fundamental. Gaining a facility with the terminology and theory that apply to your path and your goals is sufficient. And doing so will free you from the frustration, confusion, and self-doubt that plague musicians who have avoided the very skills that will help them. All that is required is effort and patience.

Theory is not just for professional musicians, just as grammar is not just for grammarians and writers. Though I feel it is especially important for anyone wanting to make a career out of music, a strong, basic understanding of the language is helpful for anyone who plays it.

In this series of lessons, I aim to introduce you to the fundamentals of music, dispel notions of it being onerous, obscure, or restrictive, and demonstrate concepts in a way that is approachable and readily applicable to the guitar. By expanding your musical education, my belief is you'll be better equipped to reach your musical goals, and my hope is it that greater fluency will foster an enhanced connection with your muses. You are a unique individual, and therefore your creative expression is unique. Give yourself all the tools—especially those within easy reach—toward developing that voice that is yours alone.

The structure of these lessons will be to go over the theory first, then explore how it applies to the guitar. I recommend *really* taking your time with the first step. Plan to read sections multiple times and review previous lessons. Prioritize depth of understanding, and be patient. This is about long-term investment, not immediate gratification. Once you're solid with the concepts, then examine them through your fingers on the fretboard.

Though this series should provide the opportunity for acquiring a strong foundation, it is merely a beginning. A person could spend a lifetime of musical study and still uncover new treasures and mysteries. See this as an introduction to a huge subject, a step on a lifelong path, should you choose.

I thank you for letting me be a small part of your musical journey. Music has one of the highest benefit-to-risk ratios out there—it has the power to delight, inspire, comfort, and unite. Yet the most common downside is that certain types might not appeal to you aesthetically. So be fearless as you learn and grow, knowing you'll harm no one. Invest in your musical fluency, cultivate your imagination, develop your sound, and create from your highest self. You never know how you might affect the world positively.

—*Gretchen Menn*

Notation Guide

In this section I'll take you through some fundamentals of notation. Though not all of it will be found in the following lessons, it will all be beneficial to know as a guitarist. Music is a language and, like many languages, has a written form. In order to be literate, one must become familiar with what each character and symbol represent.

Guitarists use several types of notation, including standard notation, tablature, and chord diagrams. Standard notation is a universal system in Western music. Becoming competent with standard notation will allow you to share and play music with almost any other instrument. Tablature is a notation system exclusively for stringed instruments with frets—like guitar and mandolin—that shows you what strings and frets to play to achieve the desired pitches. Chord diagrams use a graphic representation of the fretboard to show chord shapes on fretted instruments. Here's a primer on how to read these types of notation.

STANDARD NOTATION

Standard notation is written on a five-line staff. Notes are written in alphabetical order from A to G. Every time you pass a G note, the sequence of notes repeats, starting with A.

E F G A B C D E F G A B C D E F G A

The duration of a note is depicted by note head, stem, and flag. Though the number of beats each note represents will vary depending on the meter, the relations between note durations remain the same: a whole note (𝅝) is double the length of a half note (𝅗𝅥). A half note is double the length of a quarter note (𝅘𝅥). A quarter note is double the length of an eighth note (𝅘𝅥𝅮). An eighth note is double the length of a sixteenth note (𝅘𝅥𝅯). And so on. You'll notice each time a flag gets added, the note duration halves.

The numbers that follow the clef (4/4, 3/4, 6/8, etc.) or **C** shown at the beginning of a piece of music denote the time signature. The top number tells you how many beats are in each measure, and the bottom number indicates the rhythmic value of each beat (4 equals a quarter note, 8 equals an eighth note, 16 equals a sixteenth note, and 2 equals a half note).

The most common time signature is 4/4, which signifies four quarter notes per measure and is sometimes designated with the symbol **C** (for common time). The symbol **₵** stands for cut time (2/2). Note that while in staff notation, a time signature's two numbers are stacked vertically, in text they're expressed as fractions, for the sake of readability. But don't let that confuse you—time signatures are, indeed, not fractions. 4/4 is pronounced, "four four," not "four fourths." Likewise, 3/4 is, "three four" time, not "three fourths," or "three quarter" time.

TABLATURE

In tablature, the six horizontal lines represent the six strings of the guitar, low to high, as on the guitar. The numbers refer to fret numbers on the indicated string.

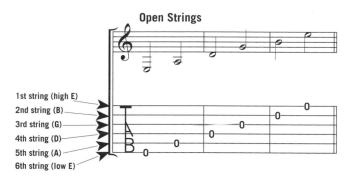

Much of this book is designed to strengthen the reading of standard notion, a notoriously weak area for guitarists. Tablature is nevertheless included as a supplement to indicate fretboard locations and implied fingerings. In order to get the most out of these lessons, I encourage you to use the standard notation as primary, referring to the tablature only as needed.

FINGERINGS

Fingerings are indicated with small numbers and letters in the notation. Fretting-hand fingering is expressed as 1 for the index finger, 2 the middle, 3 the ring, 4 the pinky, and *T* the thumb. Picking-hand fingering is conveyed by *i* for the index finger, *m* the middle, *a* the ring, *c* the pinky, and *p* the thumb.

STRUMMING AND PICKING

In music played with a flatpick, downstrokes (toward the floor) and upstrokes (toward the ceiling) are shown as follows. Slashes in the notation and tablature indicate a strum through the previously played chord.

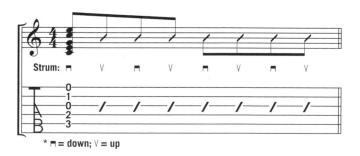

In music played with the pick-hand fingers, *split stems* are often used to highlight the division between thumb and fingers. With split stems, notes played by the thumb have stems pointing down, while notes played by the fingers have stems pointing up. If split stems are not used, pick-hand fingerings are usually present. Here is the same fingerpicking pattern shown with and without split stems. Clarity will inform which option is used.

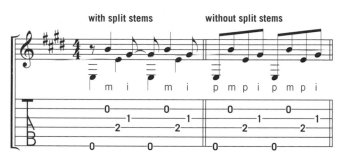

CHORD DIAGRAMS

Chord diagrams are a convenient way of depicting chord shapes. Frets are presented horizontally. The thick top line represents the nut. A fret number to the right of a diagram indicates a chord played higher up the neck (in this case the top horizontal line is thin and the fret number is designated). Strings are shown as vertical lines. The line on the far left represents the sixth (lowest) string, and the line on the far right represents the first (highest) string. Dots mark where the fingers go, and thick horizontal lines illustrate barres. Numbers above the diagram are fretting-hand finger numbers, as used in standard notation.

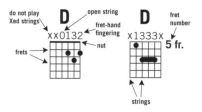

The given fingerings are only suggestions. They are generally what would most typically be considered standard. In context, however, musical passages may benefit from other fingerings for smoothest chord transitions. An X means a string that should be muted or not played; 0 indicates an open string.

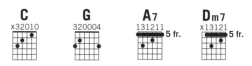

CAPOS

If a capo is used, a Roman numeral designates the fret where the capo should be placed. The standard notation and tablature is written as if the capo were the nut of the guitar. For instance, a tune capoed anywhere up the neck and played using key-of-G chord shapes and fingerings will be written in the key of G. Likewise, open strings held down by the capo are written as open strings.

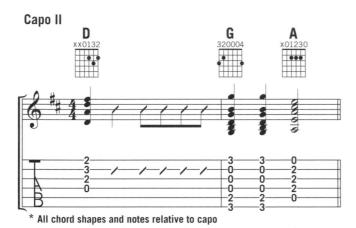

* All chord shapes and notes relative to capo

TUNINGS

Alternate tunings are given from the lowest (sixth) string to the highest (first) string. D A D G B E is standard tuning with the bottom string dropped to D. Standard notation for songs in alternate tunings always reflects the actual pitches of the notes.

VOCAL TUNES

Vocal tunes are sometimes written with a fully tabbed-out introduction and a vocal melody with chord diagrams for the rest of the piece. The tab intro is usually your clue as to which strumming or fingerpicking pattern to use in the rest of the piece. The melody with lyrics underneath is that which is sung by the vocalist. Occasionally, smaller notes are written with the melody to indicate other instruments or the harmony part sung by another vocalist. These are not to be confused with cue notes, which are small notes that express variation in melodies when a section is repeated. Listen to a recording of the piece to get a feel for the guitar accompaniment and to hear the singing if you aren't skilled at reading vocal melodies.

ARTICULATIONS

There are a number of ways you can articulate a note on the guitar. Notes connected with slurs (not to be confused with ties) in the tablature or standard notation are executed with either a hammer-on, pull-off, or slide. Lower notes slurred to higher notes are played as hammer-ons; higher notes slurred to lower notes are played as pull-offs.

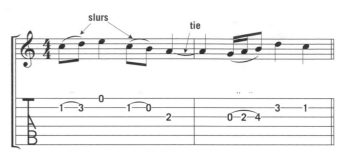

Slides are represented with a dash. A dash preceding a note is a slide into the note from an indefinite point in the direction of the slide; a dash following a note is a slide off the note to an indefinite point in the direction of the slide. For two slurred notes connected with a slide, pick the first note and then slide into the second.

Bends are denoted with upward arrows. Most bends have a specific destination pitch—the number above the bend symbol shows how much the bend raises the pitch: ¼ for a slight bend, ½ for a half step, 1 for a whole step.

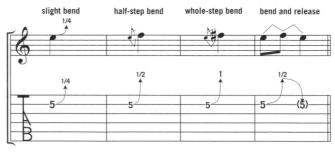

Grace notes are represented by small notes with a slash through the stem in standard notation and with small numbers in the tablature. A grace note is a quick musical ornament with no specific note value leading into a note, most commonly executed as a hammer-on, pull-off, or slide. In the first example below, pluck the note at the fifth fret on the beat, then quickly hammer onto the seventh fret. The second example is executed as a quick pull-off from the second fret to the open string. In the third example, both notes at the fifth fret are played simultaneously (even though it appears that the fourth string at the fifth fret is to be played by itself), then the fourth string, seventh fret is quickly hammered.

HARMONICS

Harmonics are expressed as diamond-shaped notes in the standard notation and a small dot next to the tablature numbers. Natural harmonics are indicated with the text "Harmonics" or "Harm." above the tablature. Harmonics articulated with the picking hand (often called artificial harmonics) include the text "R.H. Harmonics" or "R.H. Harm." above the tab. Picking-hand harmonics are executed by lightly touching the harmonic node (usually 12 frets above the open string or fretted note) with the picking hand index finger and plucking the string with the thumb, ring finger, or pick. For extended phrases played with picking-hand harmonics, the fretted notes are shown in the tab along with instructions to touch the harmonics 12 frets above the notes.

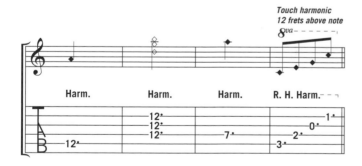

REPEATS

One of the most confusing parts of a musical score can be the navigation symbols, such as repeats, *D.S. al Coda, D.C. al Fine, To Coda*, etc. Repeat symbols are placed at the beginning and end of the passage to be repeated.

When you encounter a repeat sign, take note of the location of the begin repeat symbol (with the dots to the right of the lines), play until you reach the end repeat symbol (with the dots to the left of the lines). Then go back to the begin repeat sign, and play the section again.

If you find an end repeat only sign, go back to the beginning of the piece and repeat. The next time you get to the end repeat, continue to the next section of the piece unless there is text that specifically indicates to repeat additional times.

A section will often have a different ending after each repeat. The example below includes a first and a second ending. Play until you hit the repeat symbol, return to the begin repeat symbol, and play until you reach the bracketed first ending. Then skip the measures under the bracket and jump immediately to the second ending, and then continue.

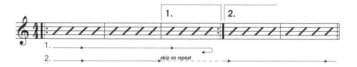

D.S. stands for *dal segno* or "from the sign." When you encounter this indication, advance immediately to the sign (𝄋). *D.S.* is usually accompanied by *al Fine* or *al Coda*. *Fine* indicates the end of a piece. A coda is a final passage near the end of a piece and is indicated with ⊕. *D.S. al Coda* simply tells you to go back to the sign and continue on until you are instructed to move to the coda, indicated with *To Coda* ⊕.

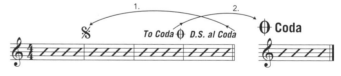

D.C. stands for *da capo* or "from the beginning." Jump to the top of the piece when you encounter this indication.

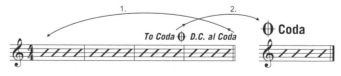

D.C. al Fine tells you to proceed to the beginning and continue until you encounter the *Fine* indicating the end of the piece (ignore the *Fine* the first time through).

Note Finder

Learning the names of the pitches on the fretboard—and on the staff

THE PROBLEM: The identity of the notes on your fretboard is a mystery. Whenever someone uses music theory terms, you feel intimidated and extricate yourself as quickly as possible from the conversation.

THE SOLUTION: Invest some time to systematically familiarize yourself with the fundamentals of music. Demystify the fretboard through applying this knowledge and building fluency.

Many guitar players are unfamiliar with at least certain parts of the fretboard. There might be a solid grasp of the low E and A strings up to 5th fret or so, but a journey to the center of the neck on higher strings may reveal uncertain territory. Yet the principles that allow us to know the notes on any string—or portion of a string—apply to all of them across the instrument. It's just a matter of taking the time and effort to continuously expand that comfort zone.

Rote memorization is a tedious and less effective method for true learning, so let's start by gaining an understanding of some primary concepts in music, then seeing how that can enhance our visualization and eventual memorization of our playground—the guitar's fretboard.

In this lesson, you'll dive into the fundamentals of pitch and apply what you learn to the guitar. If you can count to 12 and know the alphabet up to letter G, you'll be fine. There will be some terms to learn, but what's a few new words in your vocabulary, especially if they pertain to something important to you? You won't find any tablature here, as the goal is to get you comfortable with standard notation. So shed intimidation and reject the temptation to fall into the proud ignorance that persists in guitar culture. It's time to get literate in the language you love.

LEARN THE THEORY

First some terminology. Even if this is review for you, brushing up on terms ensures a recent, specific foundation as you move ahead. **Pitch** refers to the frequency of a sound. It can be expressed in Hz, or, commonly, as **notes**, which are named or notated pitches. There are 12 different notes in the Western tonal system: A, A#/Bb, B, C, C#/Db, D, D#/Eb, E, F, F#/Gb, G, and G#/Ab.

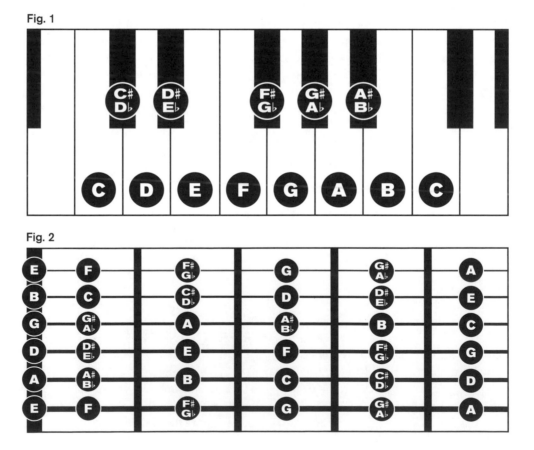

Fig. 1

Fig. 2

Notes that are represented just with a letter are known as natural notes. **Accidentals** are symbols that alter a note. A **sharp** (♯) raises a note a half step, and a **flat** (♭) lowers a note a half step. A **natural** (♮) cancels a sharp or flat. More on accidentals later, but for now just know that each accidental applies to the same note throughout a measure (as designated by the vertical lines on the staff), or until it is canceled by another accidental in the same measure.

On a piano, as shown in **Figure 1**, natural notes are the white keys, and the sharp and flat notes are the black keys. The closest distance between notes is a half step (e.g., A–A♯ or B–C). Two half steps are equivalent to a whole step (e.g., A–B or B–C♯). The guitar has a different layout from that of the piano: half steps are between adjacent frets, as demonstrated in **Figure 2**.

Notes can be interpreted in various ways, and therefore have different names, such as A♯/B♭. These are known as **enharmonic equivalents**. Context will determine which name applies. More on that later, but for now just know that A♯ is the same pitch as B♭, C♯ is equivalent to D♭, and so on.

Also notice the half steps that occur between two sets of natural notes: B–C and E–F. If you see a B♯ or E♯ in notation, they are enharmonically C and F, respectively. Similarly, C♭ and F♭ are the same as B and E.

STUDY THE STAFF

Notes are notated on a **staff**—a system of five lines and four spaces. A **clef** is a symbol that occurs at the beginning of a staff to indicate which lines and spaces are to be associated with which notes. Guitar is written in **treble clef**, also known as **G clef**, as it encircles the line associated with G above middle C. (I must mention that the guitar is written an octave above sounding pitch.)

The treble, or G, clef is the one used for standard guitar notation.

It's commonly taught to memorize the lines (E G B D F) and spaces (F A C E), as shown in **Example 1**. You can also just locate the G line as designated by the treble clef, and count up or down alphabetically. **Ledger lines**, depicted in **Example 2**, extended

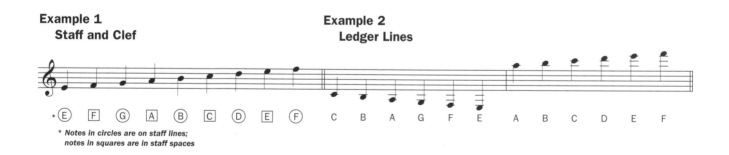

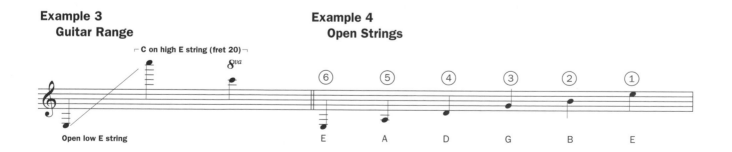

the staff upward and downward. **Example 3** shows the range of a typical 20-fret acoustic guitar, in standard tuning.

APPLY THE THEORY

With an understanding of some basics, apply that knowledge to the fretboard, and boost your fluency with some memorization drills. **Example 4** shows the six open strings— low to high, E, A, D, G, B, and E—as they appear on the staff.

The first step toward fretboard demystification is to memorize each open string. The second step is to learn the notes on each individual string. I recommend starting with the low E. You'll get two for one, as the note names will be the same as on the high E. Here's how to practice: Set a timer for 10 minutes. Focus on the notes from the open E up to the sixth fret, starting with just the open string and the first fret, and adding notes one at a time. Say them aloud as you play them.

Example 5 will get you started. Notice enharmonic equivalents, and get used to both ways of interpreting notes. This is a drill, so the idea is to work carefully on a very manageable amount of material and commit your full focus, even if it starts to feel easy. The goal isn't just to get it right, but to be unable to get it wrong. Try to come up with different combinations, or enlist a practice buddy to throw out random notes for you. When the timer goes off, you're done for the day.

Take a couple of minutes the next day to review, then work in the same way from frets 7 to 12 of the E string. The following day, start with a full review of the E string, and then tackle the first six frets of the A string. Continue in this way until you've gone through each string. Spend a few days going between strings, looking at notes in various positions, trying to disorient yourself so you can then reorient and deepen your learning.

Apply this type of note identification to melodies or licks you know. In about two weeks, and with a little over two hours invested, you should have vastly increased your confidence with notes on the fretboard.

Any path of education means a learning curve, which may feel overwhelming at times. Keep with it. Go slowly and methodically. Review and reread as often as necessary. You'll start to see the patterns and relationships that make music theory so comprehensible, so beautifully logical. And there are benefits beyond what you might expect. You've got this!

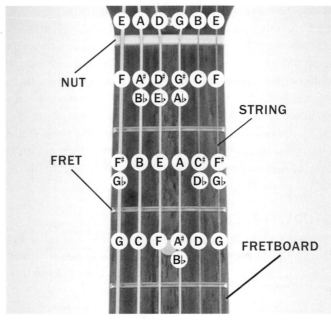

Get to know the notes on each string.

Example 5

Scale Models, Part 1
How to understand and build scales

THE PROBLEM: You're at the mercy of the scales you've memorized by rote learning or what you can decipher by ear. You don't know how the scale patterns are built, what functions the notes have, or how to transpose them.

THE SOLUTION: Look at the basics of scale formation, and then apply that knowledge to the guitar.

This lesson builds upon Note Finder. Make sure you've devoted the time to absorbing it and learning the notes on the neck. The goal of these lessons is to build a solid knowledge foundation, so I don't recommend skipping over any piece—even that which may be review. Whenever I revisit something I think I already know, I invariably reach a more nuanced insight, greater clarity, and ultimately a deeper understanding.

We begin with the theory.

A **scale** is a pattern of **intervals** that span an **octave**. An octave is the distance between two pitches—one with half or double the vibrational frequency of the other. For example, there's an octave between C and the next higher or lower C (**Fig. 1**). In Western music, the smallest interval is a half step. On guitar, that's the distance between any two adjacent frets. On a piano, it's the distance between keys right next to each other, white or black. A whole step is the equivalent of two half steps, or the distance between two frets.

LEARN THE FORMULA

The **major scale** will be your entry point for comprehending scales in general. It's a very practical place to start, as it's found everywhere. Once you've wrapped your mind around it, you'll be able to learn other scales and modes with just slight alterations to what you already know. The major scale owes its characteristic sound to a pattern of half (H) and whole steps (W): W W H W W W H. So, to spell a C major scale, start on the note C (1), add the note a whole step higher, D (2), then another whole step, E (3), and so on. The complete scale is spelled C D E F G A B C. There are seven notes which span an octave, with the **tonic**, or note from which the scale is built, starting and ending the sequence, in this case, C. All of this is shown in notation in **Example 1**.

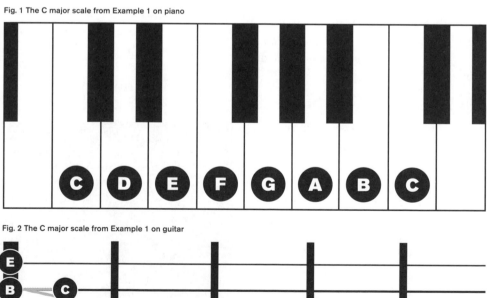

Fig. 1 The C major scale from Example 1 on piano

Fig. 2 The C major scale from Example 1 on guitar

Now spell an E major scale. Start on the first degree, E, and go up a whole step to get F♯. Remember, E–F is a half step, so add the sharp for a whole step. Add another whole step (G♯), and then continue finding the notes of the scale using the major scale pattern until you reach the tonic, E. If you applied the formula correctly, you'll arrive at this sequence of notes: E F♯ G♯ A B C♯ D♯ E.

SCALE THE HEIGHTS

Example 2 shows the E major scale played entirely on the low E string. Use the fretboard knowledge you gained from the first lesson in this series, and visualize not just each note but its relationship to the tonic (E). The purpose of playing all the notes on one string isn't because it's the most practical fingering, but so you can see most clearly how these principles apply to your instrument—and to encourage you to get out of the habit of flying through memorized shapes.

Go through the same process with the A major scale. Starting with the tonic (A), spell out the scale using the formula, and you get the following collection of notes: A B C♯ D E F♯ G♯ A. Now find those notes up the neck on the A string, as depicted in **Example 3**, before doing the same on the D, G, and B strings (**Examples 4–6**). If you like, repeat Ex. 2 on the high E string—the notes are the same, just two octaves higher.

So far you've worked only with keys in which the accidentals are sharps, so for good measure, spell an F major scale (hint: there's one flat, B♭), and play it on the sixth string, as shown in **Example 7**. When going through all of these scales, be mindful of which note is which—both in terms of note name (C, F♯, etc.) and its relation to the tonic (2, 5, etc.). And don't forget to listen carefully so that you can connect your mind, your ears, and your fingers.

EXPLORE FURTHER ON YOUR OWN

Using this same method, you can derive every other major scale. It's that easy. Just go slowly, and remember these three things:

1. The half steps that occur in a major scale are between scale degrees 3–4 and 7–8.

2. The half steps that occur between natural notes are between B–C and E–F.

3. There will be one and only one of each letter (A through G) in every major scale. So you won't have both the notes G♭ and G, for example, but F♯ (the enharmonic equivalent of G♭) and G.

Later I'll explain how you can express the major scale in finger-friendly shapes all over the fretboard. Until then, your mission, should you choose to accept it, is to find scale patterns for yourself, using this process:

1. Pick a scale—start with C major.

2. Write down the scale pattern with scale degree numbers and half steps marked with a ∨ between scale degrees 3 and 4 and 7 and 8. Then label the note name above each scale degree.

3. Transfer the note names to notation on a staff.

4. Grab your guitar, start on the low E string, and map out all of the notes in the C major scale in the open position using two or three notes per string, as shown in **Example 8**.

5. Once you're sure of the notes, find comfortable fingerings. Play the scale ascending and descending. Come up with melodic ideas within it.

6. Move up to the next note in the scale—in this case the fourth scale degree of C major, F on fret 1 of the E string. With your first finger on F, find the notes of the scale across the strings, again using two or three notes per string, and using no open strings (**Example 9**). If you forget which note you're on, work it out using your knowledge of the fretboard. The more often you can challenge yourself to reorient when you get disoriented, the more intensely you'll be learning.

There are half steps between the natural notes B and C and E and F.

7. Continue to work out the patterns starting on each note of the scale and moving up the neck so you cover each position. Try starting on different fingers and see how new shapes and patterns unfold. Then try doing the same thing in different keys. You will—and should—eventually memorize each pattern. But going about it this way means it will be an outgrowth of actual understanding. And it will be so much more meaningful, memorable, and ultimately useful.

Example 1
C Major Scale

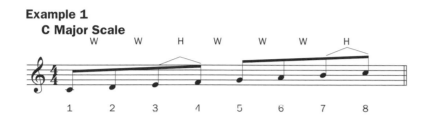

Example 2
E Major Scale

Example 3
A Major Scale

Example 4
D Major Scale

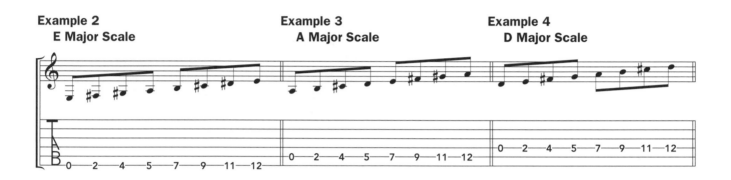

Example 5
G Major Scale

Example 6
B Major Scale

Example 7
F Major Scale

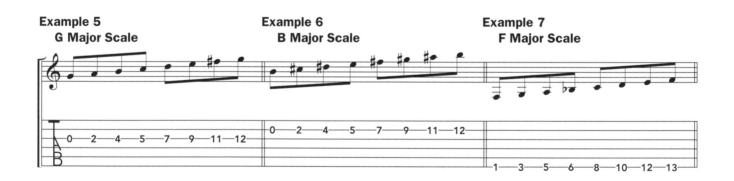

Example 8
C Major in the open position, starting on the third, E

Example 9
C Major in the first position, starting on the fourth, F

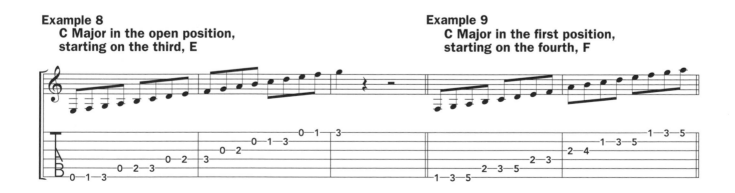

Scale Models, Part 2
More on how to build scales

THE PROBLEM: You've developed a basic familiarity with major scales, but have yet to get them completely under your fingers across the neck—or apply what you've learned toward the natural minor scale.

THE SOLUTION: Study the major scales in each position, then use that as a basis to systematically approach the minor scale.

This lesson expands on your introduction to the major scale, our foundation for learning every other mode. Your assignment was to take the concepts discussed and discover your own scalar shapes. If you haven't done this already, I can't stress enough how important the process is. Having the shapes be an outgrowth of your assimilation of the material ensures a host of benefits: You strengthen your knowledge of the fretboard and put it to practical use, you reinforce your proficiency with major scales through having to form them, and you develop the ability to reconstruct scales and shapes on the fly through your grasp of the theory.

We live in an era that places a premium on immediate gratification, which can be detrimental to deeper learning. Let me invoke your patience. After all, if you're going to spend *any* time learning scales, why not *really* learn them? Why not *own* them? In the long run it'll be a much better use of your time than glossing over an opportunity to grow as a musician.

CHECK IN WITH THE MAJOR SCALES
After all the cautionary words about why you should figure these out for yourself, **Example 1** shows some useful fingerings for the major scale: 1 = first (index) finger, 2 = second (middle), 3 = third (ring), 4 = fourth (pinky), and 0 = open string. Use these fingerings as a reference to compare with your independent study.

As you go through each pattern, don't let your mind get lazy and lapse into purely mechanical thinking. Really know each note and how it relates to the scale. Play the patterns descending as well as ascending. Isolate sections and create melodic lines within them. Jump between scale degrees and strings.

SEE THE CONNECTIONS
The beauty of being familiar with both the theory and the fretboard is that you'll be eligible for a 12-for-the-price-of-one deal: Learn the fingerings for C major, and you'll be able to apply them to all 12 keys. All the scale shapes (with the exception of the first shape, in open position) are moveable—in any other major key, these same patterns will apply. You'll just have to transpose them, reorienting around your new key center. **Example 2** uses the F major scale to get you started with this

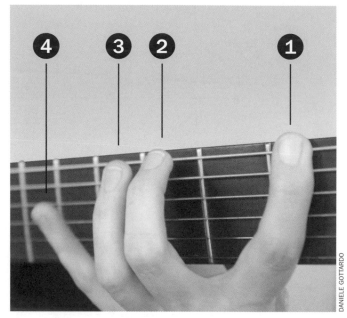

Finger numbers for the fretting hand.

concept. First, find the notes in F major by applying the pattern of half and whole steps you learned on page 13 to get the following note collection: F G A B♭ C D E F.

Then go to the F on the first fret of the E string and spell out the scale. Does it look familiar? Compare it to C major starting on C of the E string. This is your form for a major scale starting with the root on the low E string. Now try it starting on the second degree (G), as shown in bars 3–4 of Ex. 2, and then moving up the fretboard (not shown in notation). As you connect the F major scale in various positions, you should find that you already know the shapes.

Want to play an A major scale starting on the root? No problem. Find the A on your E string, use the major scale fingering you now know, and there you go. In looking at scales this way, I would strongly urge you to resist the temptation to think exclusively in terms of finger patterns. Instead, maintain active focus by saying the notes aloud as you play them. Skip between notes, challenging your knowledge of both the scale and fretboard. And always remember to engage your ear by paying attention to what each note sounds like within the context of the key.

KNOW YOUR KEY SIGNATURES
As you start exploring keys with more sharps and flats, you'll see why **key signatures** are so useful. In conventional notation, a key signature is displayed at the beginning of each staff of music, just to the right of the clef and to the left of the time signature. A key signature expresses which notes are to have sharps or flats, unless otherwise

Example 1

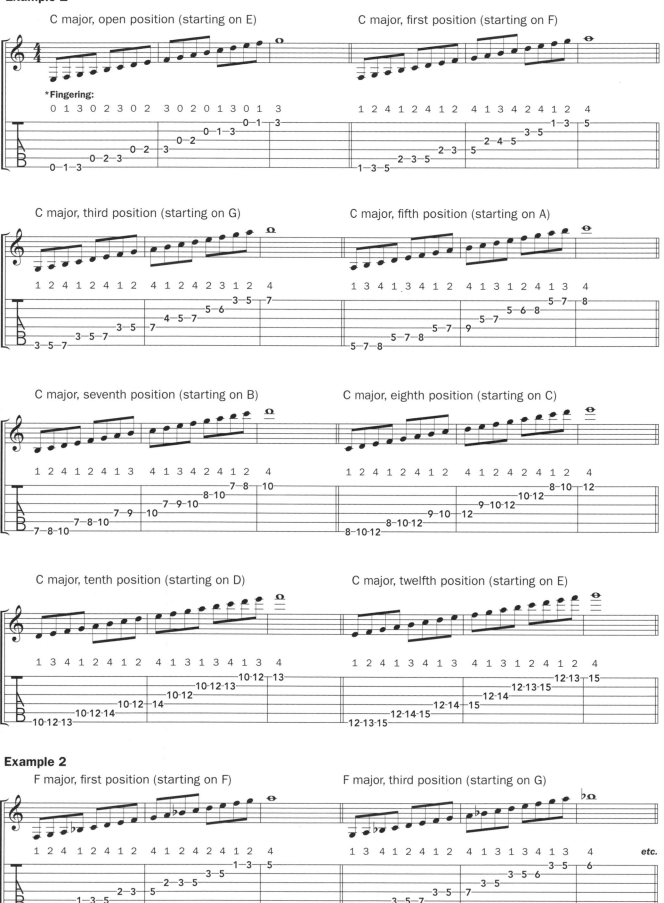

Example 2

indicated with an accidental (sharp or ♯, flat or ♭, natural or ♮). Key signatures alleviate the burden of writing out every sharp or flat inherent in a given key, and also allow you to easily identify the key of a piece simply by looking at the key signature.

Figure 1 shows the various sharp and flat key signatures, both major and minor. Notice that for every major key, there is a minor key with the same key signature. That is not to be confused with being the same key—they each have their own tonal center and associated chord progressions. More on that later, but the fact that they share all the same notes makes them **relative keys**.

Here's a quick way to know which major key is associated with a key signature: For sharp keys, the key is a half-step up from the last sharp. So if the last sharp in the key signature is C♯, go up a half step to get the key of D major. For flat keys, the key is the second to the last flat. Using this method, the only two key signatures you have to memorize outright are C major (no sharps or flats) and F major (one flat).

GET INTO THE MINOR MODE

Just as the characteristic sound of the major scale comes from its pattern of half and whole steps, so does that of the minor, often called natural minor to differentiate it from altered versions. In this scale, the half steps occur between degrees 2–3 and 5–6. So if you start on A, you get A B C D E F G A. Look like the same notes of any other scale you know? No sharps or flats means it shares the same notes as C major, which is the relative major of A minor. With that big clue to fuel you, I encourage you to work out the minor scales the same way you approached the major scales. You should now be able to get started on your own. We will add one slight variation to tune your ear: play the tonic minor chord before and after each scale. This will help you hear the minor key, rather than the relative major.

The process is:

1. Pick a scale—start with A minor.

2. Write down the scale pattern with scale degree numbers and corresponding half and whole steps. Then input the note names above each scale degree.

3. Transfer the note names to notation on a staff.

4. Grab your guitar and play an A minor chord. Then, starting on the low E string, map out all of the notes in the A minor scale in the open position using two or three notes per string. End by playing an A minor chord again.

5. Once you're sure of the notes, find comfortable fingerings.

6. Move up to the next note in A minor, the F at the first fret of the E string. With your first finger on F, build the scale across the strings, again using two or three notes per string, and no open strings.

7. Continue to find the patterns starting on each note of the scale, moving up the neck so you cover each position. Notice how they are the same patterns as the C major scale, but with a different tonal center: What was C major starting on the sixth scale degree now becomes the A minor scale starting on the root, and what was C major starting on the root is A minor starting on the third. Don't be afraid to read that again and do some fretboard experiments to prove it to yourself.

If, as you diligently familiarize yourself with the minor scale shapes, you find yourself considering throwing in the towel and sneaking a peek at fingerings or shapes someone else has worked out for you, turn to this proverb for strength: "I hear, and I forget. I see, and I remember. I do, and I understand." Put in the time and mental effort and devote your attention to the task at hand. It will be well worth it.

Figure 1
Key Signatures

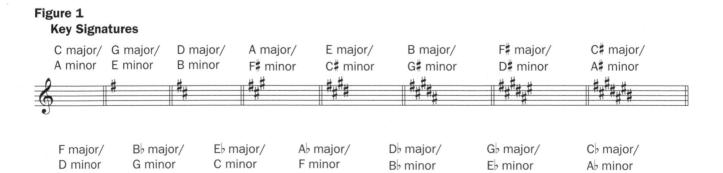

Get Rhythm, Part 1

Beats, meters, and more

THE PROBLEM: Rhythm is a shaky area for you. You have a difficult time communicating a rhythmic idea unless you can play it. You have a tendency to fall into familiar, repetitive patterns.

THE SOLUTION: Learn the fundamentals of rhythm, then work through exercises designed to improve your rhythmic cognition.

Music takes place in time. Nothing is more fundamental to music than its temporal aspect. Becoming versed in elements of rhythm will strengthen not only your sense of time but also your phrasing and how you feel accents and syncopations. And it will open creative doors by increasing your musical vocabulary, leading to greater nuance and variety in your playing.

LEARN THE TERMINOLOGY

Beat refers to the pulse of music. A simple way to find the beat of a particular piece or passage is to tap your foot in time to the music. **Tempo** is how quickly these beats occur and is usually written above the staff, with a directive like *Lento, Allegro, Presto,* or a metronome mark, specifying the number of beats per minute (bpm).

Meter is the grouping of beats into **measures**, which are shown by vertical lines across the staff. In general, the first beat of a measure has a particular sense of weight or accent. The most standard groupings are duple (grouped in two, counted *1, 2*), triple (grouped in three, counted *1, 2, 3*), or quadruple meter (grouped in four, counted *1, 2, 3, 4*). There are many other meters, but to start, it's best to focus on the most essential. Once you have your head around the concept of meter you'll be on solid ground for assimilating more complex structures.

Meter is depicted at the beginning of a piece by a **time signature**—two numbers arranged vertically. The top number specifies how many beats are in a measure; the lower number designates which duration of note represents one beat. So 4/4—a meter so ubiquitous it is also designated by C, for common time—means there are four beats per measure (quadruple meter) with the quarter note receiving one beat. The symbol 2/2 means two beats per measure (duple meter, or cut time), with the half note receiving one beat. Don't let the way meters are often written in text confuse you. They are not fractions. 4/4 time is correctly read, "four four." 3/4 time is "three four"—not "three fourths" or "three quarters."

GET VISUAL

Example 1 shows how basic note values and rests are represented visually. The numbers below the music show the relationships between the note and rest durations and the beats in the measure. The numbers are just to get you

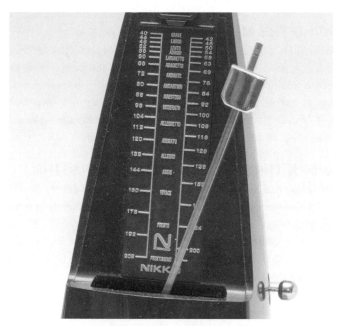

A metronome is an indispensable tool for developing a solid sense of rhythm.

started visualizing. They are not part of standard rhythmic notation. Note that two or more consecutive eighth or 16th notes are often beamed together with horizontal lines, as shown in measure 5 of Ex. 1. An individual eighth note gets one flag, or curved top, as in the first bar of the next example, while a 16th gets two flags, as appearing throughout the last example of this lesson.

In **Example 2**, you'll find some ties. A tie connects two or more notes, creating a duration equal to their sum. A dot next to a note adds half the note's value to itself (**Example 3**).

Now try a counting exercise, as shown in **Example 4**. Set a metronome to 50 bpm. With your right hand, tap along with the click. As you look at the measure, mentally divide it into the number of pulses it contains—in this case, four. As you tap, visualize where each beat is in the measure. This will help you keep your place as you become accustomed to reading music in real time. With your left hand, tap the written note value. Count the durations out loud—not in your head, but actually saying them. For rests, continue to tap the pulse and count the values, but don't tap with the hand designated for notes.

Once you've finished the exercise, switch hands and repeat it. You'll become ambidextrous right from the beginning. Remember that rhythm is perceived by a combination of sounds and silences, so pay as much attention to rests as to notes.

PICK UP YOUR GUITAR

Once you feel confident negotiating the rhythms in Ex. 4, try them on your guitar. Set your metronome at about 50 bpm.

Only move to quicker tempos once you've mastered the slower tempos. Tap your foot with the beats of the metronome, play the notes, and count out loud. Though I have randomly picked the note C, you can use any note on the neck to play the example.

MIND THE METERS

Now take a quick look at hearing and playing in three frequently used meters (**Example 5**). Set your metronome to about 80 bpm. As in Ex. 4, tap the pulse with your right hand. Count out loud, emphasizing the *one*. Then, tapping your foot with the metronome and counting out loud, play the notes on the guitar, emphasizing the notes that fall on the 1.

WORK THROUGH A PLETHORA OF 16THS

Example 6, which explores various 16th-note patterns, should keep you busy for quite a while. I recommend spending time on it daily until you fully internalize the various rhythms. Begin with a very slow metronome setting. As before, work first on counting. Tap with one hand, in the smallest subdivision of the beat—in this case, the 16th note. With your other hand, tap the written rhythm while counting out loud. You could find virtually endless permutations by incorporating other note values. The focus here is on the 16th note because that rhythmic unit is a very useful subdivision to master. If you can nail these rhythms, patterns with whole, half, quarter, and eighth notes will be no problem. After you have spent time with saying and tapping the rhythms, pick up your guitar and play them. Tap your foot with the pulse of the metronome (quarter notes, not 16ths), play the patterns on your guitar, and count out loud.

This rhythm lesson may be a mere introduction to an enormous topic, but the journey of a thousand miles begins with one step. With a little work invested, the next time your teacher or music buddy tells you to start a phrase on the second 16th note of the first beat of the measure in 3/4, you'll know exactly what they mean—and you'll be able to play it.

Tapping your foot, with or without a metronome, is an excellent way to keep time.

Example 1

Example 2

Example 3

Example 4

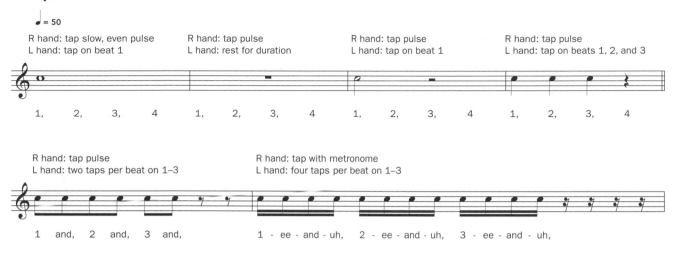

Example 5

Example 6

Get Rhythm, Part 2
Deeper into beats, meters, and other fundamentals

In the previous chapter, I covered some necessary terminology, introduced basic note values, and provided a number of musical examples, both for counting and for playing on the guitar. I suggest taking a moment to review the associated examples. Even if this feels unnecessary, it's always a good idea to revisit the basics—not only to further solidify the foundation upon which all else is built, but to provide new insights as you examine something familiar with fresh eyes and skills.

DOTTED RHYTHMS

As you saw in Part 1, a dot next to a note adds half the note value to its length. So the duration of a dotted half note is a half note plus a quarter note. A dotted quarter note is a quarter plus an eighth note. A dotted eighth note is an eighth plus a 16th. As previously, you'll start by internalizing and counting the rhythms, then applying them to the guitar.

Example 1a depicts a dotted-quarter rhythm in 4/4: a quarter note plus eighth. Tap the smallest subdivision of the beat—in this case, the eighth note—at a slow tempo with your right hand. Use a metronome if you'd like, but it's also fine to tap a slow, manageable tempo. Count out loud: *1* and, *2 and*, *3* and, *4 and*. With your left hand, tap the rhythm as indicated in italics. Be sure to look at the notated rhythm once you understand it—don't focus on the written words. They are there to get you started, but you'll want to get comfortable with notated music.

The positions of the eighth and dotted quarter notes are reversed in Example 1b. Here, tap *1 and*, 2 and, *3 and*, 4 and. In Examples 1c–1d, the note values from the previous two figures are halved. For Example 1c, featuring the rhythm of a dotted eighth note followed by a 16th, tap the smallest subdivision of the beat—the 16th note—with your hand. Count aloud and tap *1*-ee-and-*ah*, *2*-ee-and-*ah*, *3*-ee-and-*ah*, *4*-ee-and-*ah*. Example 1d, reverses the dotted eighth–16th rhythm: *1*-ee-and-ah, *2*-ee-and-ah, *3*-ee-and-ah, *4*-ee-and-ah.

Once you're comfortable saying and tapping these rhythms, grab your guitar and play them, tapping your foot in quarter notes, but using the same verbal counting as when you tap the rhythms with your hands. Choose whatever chord or note you feel like. The idea is to pick something easy for your fretting hand so you can focus your attention on the rhythms.

TIED RHYTHMS

A **tie**—a curved line connecting two or more notes—creates a note value equal to the sum of the notes. Ties can join notes of any value, and in some cases ties function similarly to dots. For in-

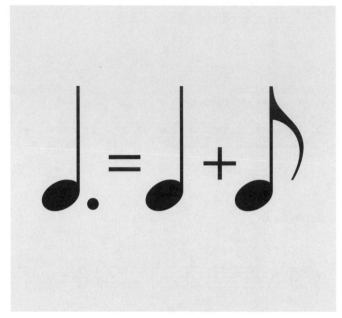

A dotted quarter note is equal to a quarter note plus an eighth.

stance, Ex. 1b could be alternatively notated as shown in **Example 2a**. Though the two figures are rhythmically identical, Ex. 2a makes it easier to visually interpret each beat of the measure.

Example 2b shows a quarter note tied to the first 16th of the following beat. To negotiate this figure, tap the smallest subdivision with your right hand, while counting out loud and tapping with your left hand: *1*-ee-and-ah, *2-ee-and-ah*, *3*-ee-and-ah, *4-ee-and-ah*. Work out **Example 2c**, which builds upon Ex. 2b, with your left hand tapping *1*-ee-*and*-ah, *2-ee-and-ah*, *3*-ee-*and*-ah, *4-ee-and-ah*. A new rhythm—the dotted eighth, followed by a 16th tied to an eighth—is introduced in **Example 2d**. Count it like this: *1*-ee-and-*ah*, *2-ee-and-ah*, *3*-ee-and-*ah,* *4-ee-and-ah*. As with all examples, when you feel confident, transfer them to the guitar.

TRIPLETS AND TUPLETS

A **tuplet** is any rhythm that divides the beat into an equal number of subdivisions other than implied by the meter. The most common type of tuplet in simple meter is the **triplet**—three equal notes in the space normally occupied by two, indicated with a numeric 3 either above or below the group of notes, which are sometimes bracketed. Given the underlying pulse of a quarter note, as in 3/4 or 4/4 time, eighth-note triplets would mean three notes per beat, rather than the typical two. Similarly, 16th-note triplets are three per eighth note (or six per quarter).

Example 3a shows one measure of eighth-note triplets. First, try counting them. In this case, it will make it most comprehensible to count and tap quarter notes with your right hand, and as follows with your left hand: *1-2-3* or *1-trip-let*. For

Example 1a

Example 1b

Count: *1* and, *2* *and,* *3* and, *4* *and* *1* and, *2* *and,* *3* *and,* *4* and

Example 1c

Example 1d

1 - ee-and-*ah,* *2* - ee-and-*ah,* *3* - ee-and-*ah,* *4* - ee-and-*ah* *1* - ee-and-ah, *2* - ee-and-ah, *3* - cc-and-ah, *4* - ee-and-ah

Example 2a

Example 2b

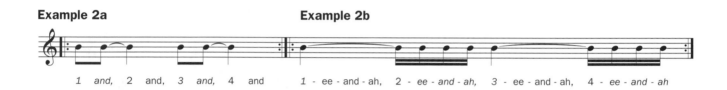

1 *and,* *2* and, *3* *and,* *4* and *1* - ee - and - ah, *2* - ee - and - ah, *3* - ee - and - ah, *4* - ee - and - ah

Example 2c

Example 2d

1 - ee-and-ah, *2* - ee-and-ah, *3* - ee-and-ah, *4* - ee-and-ah *1* - ee-and-ah, *2* - ee-and-*ah,* *3* - ee-and-ah, *4* - ee-and-ah

Example 3a

Example 3b

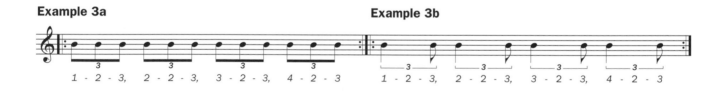

1 - 2 - 3, 2 - 2 - 3, 3 - 2 - 3, 4 - 2 - 3 1 - 2 - 3, 2 - 2 - 3, 3 - 2 - 3, 4 - 2 - 3

Example 3c

1 - 2 - 3, 1 - 2 - 3, 1 - 2 - 3, 1 - 2 - 3, 1 - 2 - 3, 1 - 2 - 3, 1 - 2 - 3, 1 - 2 - 3
Or **1** - trip - let, **2** - trip - let, etc.

Example 3d

1 - 2 - 3, 1 - 2 - 3, 1 - 2 - 3, 1 - 2 - 3, 1 - 2 - 3, 1 - 2 - 3, 1 - 2 - 3, 1 - 2 - 3
Or **1** - **2** - **3** - **4** - **5** - **6**, etc.

Example 4a **Example 4b** **Example 4c**

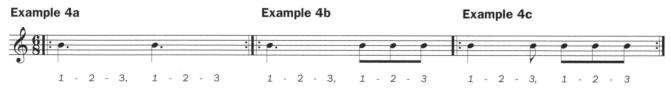

1 - *2* - *3,* *1* - *2* - *3* *1* - *2* - *3,* *1* - *2* - *3* *1* - *2* - *3,* *1* - *2* - *3*

Example 3b, containing a triplet rhythm of a quarter note followed by an eighth note, tap quarter notes with your right hand, and this pattern with your left hand: *1-2-3*, etc.

Example 3c introduces 16th-note triplets. Tap eighth notes with your right hand and triplets with your left. Because of the high number of notes per beat, I find it's more practical just to count triplets, rather than triplets and beats of the measure, like this: *1-2-3, 1-2-3,* etc. **Example 3d** shows how consecutive 16th-note triplets are more commonly expressed—as **sextuplets**, depicted with a numeric 6. Count these the same way as Ex. 3c or *1-2-3-4-5-6*.

Triplets are a good entry point to understanding and feeling **compound meters**, in which the beat consistently divides into three equal parts. In a compound meter, the note value representing one beat is a dotted note. As in simple meter, there are duple, triple, and quadruple compound meters: 6/8, 9/8, and 12/8, respectively. The top note designates the number of divisions of the beat in a measure, while the bottom number indicates which note is the division duration. So in 6/8, 9/8, or 12/8, time, that is the dotted quarter note or three eighth notes.

Example 4a shows one measure in 6/8, which I prefer to count as *1, 2, 3, 1, 2, 3*. Try the same approach to understand **Example 4b**, which juxtaposes rhythmic values, as well as **Example 4c**. The same principles apply for counting and playing in 9/8 or 12/8— there would just be more beats in each measure.

I should mention that counting/tapping isn't a strict science, and there are multiple effective ways to do so.

Some people prefer to count triplets as *tri-pul-let*; some count 6/8 as *1, 2, 3, 4, 5, 6*. Go with whatever approach makes sense and feels practical to you.

As with all the examples, study these concepts first, play them on the guitar, and then put them to use by writing something new using them. Doing so ensures they become part of your musical vocabulary. You'll not only understand the theory better, but you'll be using it to broaden your creative palette.

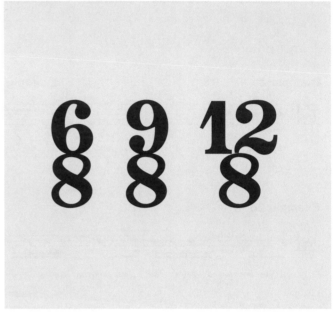

A trio of compound meters.

How to Improve Your Rhythm Playing
5 ways to build your rhythmic rudiments

Now that you've spent some time understanding fundamental rhythmic concepts and counting exercises, let's take things to the next level by going through a focused rhythm practice.

THE PROBLEM: You've studied the elements of rhythm but need to expand their application to the guitar and to your creativity.

THE SOLUTION: Put yourself through a concentrated course of rhythm boot camp.

Rhythm is one of the most essential, yet often overlooked, areas of guitar playing. Think Malcolm Young—his sense of clear, confident time is an essential part of AC/DC's sound and gave brother Angus the energetic, rock-solid foundation for blazing solos. Think Tommy Emmanuel—his virtuosic leads drop jaws, but his rhythm playing is what allows a single acoustic guitar to fill a concert hall and deliver compelling songs. And what would Led Zeppelin's "Ramble On" or "Bron-Y-Aur Stomp" be without Jimmy Page driving the rhythm?

Guitar players frequently spend a lot of energy working on lead playing and perfecting single-note technical exercises. Yet developing a strong sense of time and rhythmic vocabulary won't just make you a better rhythm player it will give your leads more rhythmic interest and variety, and make you a better musician overall.

1. GET A METRONOME

Initially, I saw my metronome as tyrannical. But when I accepted it as a mandatory part of my musical growth and re-evaluated how I was using it, my attitude changed entirely. I isolated my focus to my picking hand by muting the strings with my fretting hand. I set the metronome to 60 bpm. I played the rudiments in the following examples for at least one minute each, longer on subdivisions that were more challenging. If a full minute seems excessive for something that should be easy, keep in mind that you'll start hearing and feeling time in a deeper way only when you have the mental space to work on playing better, rather than faster or more complex. Concentrate on having a solid attack, feeling settled with the beat, and developing a sense of command and ease.

Staying with the metronome requires listening to both it and yourself. If you notice you are wandering out of synch, try to regain the beat without stopping, devoting more attention to the click of the metronome.

2. GO TO RHYTHMIC BOOT CAMP

Get in the zone with quarter notes. For all of these boot camp exercises, you will be approaching the guitar as a purely per-

Tommy Emmanuel

cussive instrument, and therefore muting the strings with the fretting hand. Play quarter notes, one strum per click, using downstrokes exclusively (**Example 1**). Examples 1-12 are expressed purely as rhythmic notation, hence no staff is necessary, as pitch information is irrelevant here. This first minute on quarter notes is when I'll close my eyes, consider my attack, and try to internalize the beat. Then check your upstrokes with eighth notes—play two notes per click of the metronome (**Example 2**), using a down-up picking pattern (down picks on downbeats). Downstrokes are naturally stronger—they have both physiology and gravity working for them. Use your ears, as it may mean consciously exaggerating the upstrokes for them to sound truly in balance. Then leave out the first eighth note, and play just the upbeats (**Example 3**).

Now mix up your pick direction with triplets, three evenly spaced notes per beat (**Example 4**). Playing triplets, or any odd subdivision of the beat, means the pick changes direction with every new group. For example, the first group would be down-up-down, then up-down-up, and so forth. It can feel inside-out to play a downbeat with an upstroke, but once you realize *why* it feels weird, working out the problem becomes a matter of listening carefully and feeling the change of where the beat falls within your picking pattern. I found it helpful to exaggerate the first note of every triplet group to maintain a sense of the downbeat. Next, leave out the first note of each triplet (**Example 5**). Keep your picking hand moving in the triplet pattern, but don't hit the strings on what would be the first note of each group. Now leave

Playing with a competent drummer is a surefire way to strengthen your sense of rhythm.

out the second note of each triplet (**Example 6**). This may feel strange, as the picking pattern is down, down, then up, up, and so on. But once your ear starts hearing it as a shuffle, that classic blues/R&B rhythm, your body will embrace it more readily.   Finally, leave out the third note of each triplet (**Example 7**). Continue with 16th notes. Play four notes per beat (**Example 8**). Then leave out the first 16th note of each group (**Example 9**), the second 16th note (Ex. 10), the third (**Example 11**), and the fourth (**Example 12**).

This boot camp requires 12 minutes of practice allocated to intense focus on rhythmic rudiments. I encourage you also to explore quintuplets, sextuplets, and septuplets (five, six, and seven notes per beat, respectively). You could get extremely geeky and continue the process of leaving out certain notes within those subdivisions, but see what feels interesting to you and pertinent to your goals.

3. MIX UP THE SUBDIVISIONS

Once you're comfortable with Examples 1 through 12, start inventing different groupings—place a few 16th notes within an eighth-note pattern, or intersperse triplets. In general, the picking hand will move with the shortest subdivision of the beat. By playing the eighth notes with two downstrokes, as in **Example 13**, your picking hand is already moving in 16th notes, which will solidify your rhythm and make the 16th notes within the phrase feel natural.

4. ADD CHORD ACCENTS

Example 14 builds upon Ex. 13 by taking the same rhythm and adding chord accents to the muted notes. I've chosen three familiar open chords—A minor, D minor, and E. Once you get confident moving between muted strums and chord accents, try adding different chords within a pattern of your own to create a riff or progression.

5. ENLIST A DRUMMER

In my experience, drummers really appreciate guitar players who want to focus more on rhythm playing, and they are often thrilled to practice their rudiments alongside some harmonic interest. So chances are you could enlist a practice buddy who rules the rhythm section and might be able to give some helpful suggestions.

BONUS TIP

With every lesson, one of the strongest pieces of advice I can offer is to write with a new concept. Making it your own and incorporating it into your immediate vocabulary will be one of the best paths to a more thorough understanding and true assimilation. Russian director Andrei Tarkovsky (*Solaris*) referred to filmmaking as "sculpting in time," and music inhabits the same dimension—sounds and silences within the framework of time. Time is your canvas. Know it and use it well.

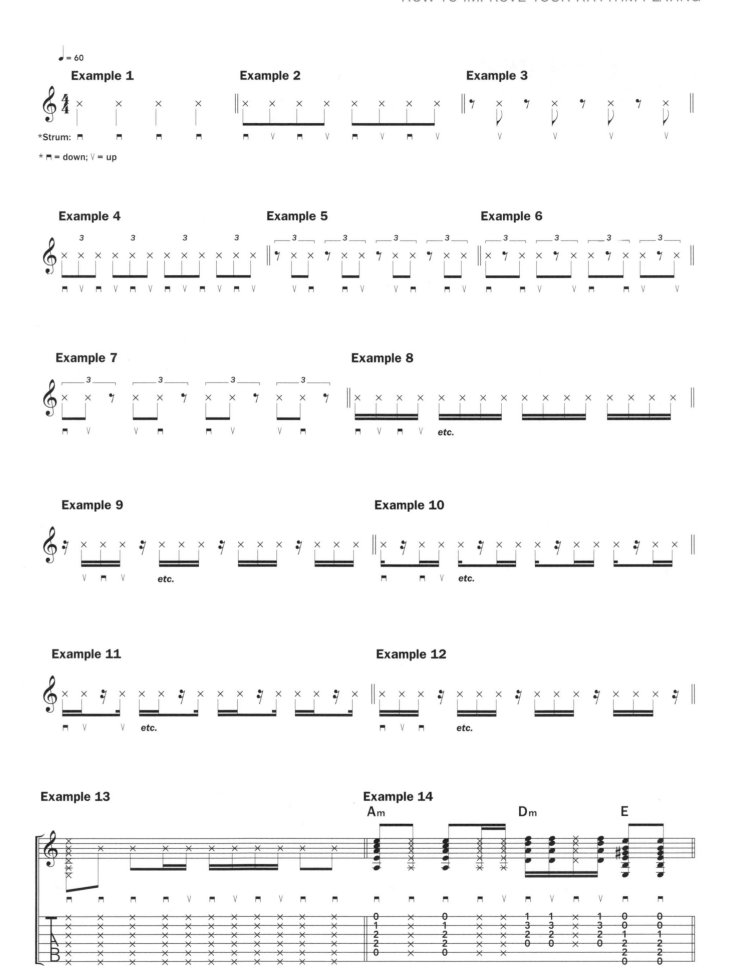

Chord Builder

Don't just memorize grips—learn to understand how harmony works

THE PROBLEM: You've memorized some chord shapes, but are unfamiliar with the theory behind their construction or how to transpose, invert, or modify them.

THE SOLUTION: Start with examining chord theory, and then apply that knowledge to the fretboard.

We often begin our journey on guitar by learning the basic open chords, and why not? The guitar is a wonderfully flexible instrument that allows for full, rich harmonies with easy fingerings. Yet many guitarists stop there. They memorize a handful of shapes, maybe a few barre chords, and rob themselves of boundless options right under their fingertips. As in all lessons in this series, we will aim to dismantle a limitation by building a strong foundation of understanding.

Full disclosure: This is a dense lesson. If you've been keeping up with the recommended assignments and made it this far, you'll be well-equipped. But don't be afraid to take a little extra time to digest the concepts and review as much as you need to feel confident prior to starting this section.

UNDERSTAND THE BUILDING BLOCKS ON THE STAFF

Before we examine chord construction, we first need to take a look at **intervals**, the distances between notes and the building blocks of chords. **Harmonic intervals** are notes played simultaneously, and **melodic intervals** are notes played in succession. Intervals are made up of two parts—a numeric distance and a preceding modifier. The numeric portion can be a unison, a second, third, fourth, fifth, sixth, seventh, or octave (**Example 1**). Intervals have one of five qualities, with abbreviations shown in parentheses: **perfect** (P), **major** (M), **minor** (m), **augmented** (+), and **diminished** (°).

Figure 1
diminished — minor — major — augmented
diminished — perfect — augmented

Figure 1 shows how intervals compress and expand to form new qualities. Diminished expanded by a half step becomes minor; minor expanded by a half step becomes major; major expanded by a half step becomes augmented. For perfect intervals, they compress and expand to form diminished and augmented intervals, respectively.

Let's use the familiar major and natural minor scales as a basis for seeing intervals in context, upwards from the root in the keys of C major (**Example 2**) and C minor (**Example 3**).

The notes C, E, and G are stacked to form a C major triad, while A, C, and E make an A minor triad.

Notice that the perfect intervals are the same in both the major and minor modes: unison (P1), perfect fourth (P4), perfect fifth (P5), and octave (P8).

The major and minor intervals are the second, third, sixth, and seventh. Both major and minor scales have a major 2nd (M2) between the root and the second scale degree. The third, sixth, and seventh are the notes that differ between the two modes. That means that in addition to building a minor scale from the associated pattern of half and whole steps, you can form it by taking the major scale and lowering the third, sixth, and seventh scale degrees a half step.

All intervals have levels of **consonance** or **dissonance**, musical rest or tension. The perfect consonances—the unison, P5, P8—have the least tension. **Imperfect consonances** are major and minor third and sixth. The P4 is a bit of a hybrid—context determines if we hear it as consonant or mildly dissonant. The M2 and m7 are **mild dissonances**, and the m2, M7, and **tritone** are **strong dissonances**. The tritone (or +4/°5) divides an octave in half.

Intervals can be **inverted**—the top and bottom note switching places, as shown in Example 4. A way to quickly calculate the new interval formed by inversion is to subtract the original interval from the number nine and flip the quality—major becomes minor (and vice versa), perfect remains perfect, and augmented becomes diminished (and vice versa). So a m2 inverts to a M7 (9 − 2 = 7; minor becomes major).

Example 1

Example 2 – C Major

Example 3 – C Minor

Example 4

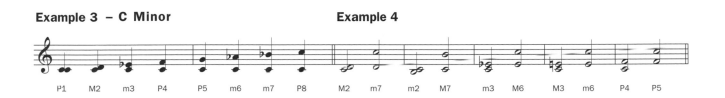

Example 5

Example 6

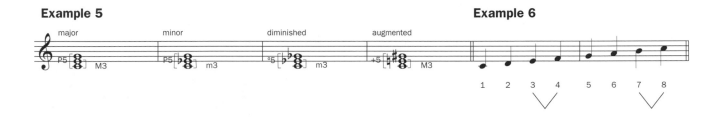

Examples 7a–d

Example 8

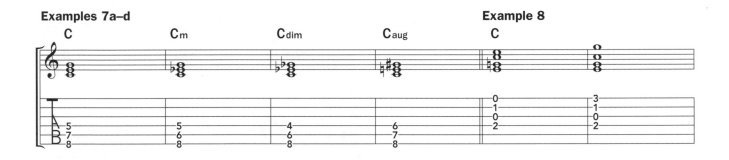

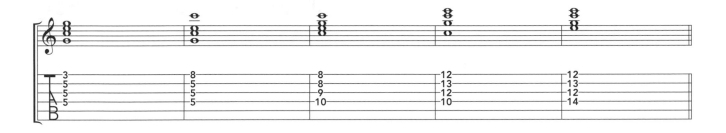

BUILD SOME TRIADS

Now let's examine chords in their fundamental form, **triads**, made up of three notes— a root, a third, and a fifth. A triad can be major, minor, augmented, or diminished, and its intervallic structure determines which (**Example 5**). A major triad has a M3 and a P5 above the root. A minor triad has a m3 and a P5. An augmented triad has a M3 and an +5. A diminished triad has a m3 and a °5.

Put this to practical use by forming various triads with C as the root. First write out the C major scale, as in **Example 6**. Find the major third above the root. Take a moment to see it both as the third degree of the C major scale and as an interval: a M3 is two whole steps—C, whole step up to D, whole step up to E, our major third. Now we need our fifth. Scale degree 5 in a major (or minor) scale is a P5 up from the root. That gives us G as the fifth. Considering it in terms of intervals, a P5 is M3 + m3 (or m3 + M3). So our C major triad is: C–E–G.

Let's transform the C triad to minor: C, a whole step up, to D, and an additional half step to E♭. We still need a P5, so our C minor triad is C–E♭–G. Notice that the only difference between C major and C minor is the third. The same is true across all major and minor chords—the third determines the chord quality.

Augmented and diminished chords are one more step: To form an augmented triad, take a major triad and raise the 5th a half step: C–E–G♯. To get a diminished triad, take a minor triad and lower the 5th by a half step: C–E♭–G♭.

TAKE IT TO THE FRETBOARD

For **Example 7a**, locate a C on the low E string. Then find the major third (E) on the A string and the fifth (G) on the D string. C major! Next, lower the third a half step, to E♭, to transform it to C minor, as shown in **Example 7b**. Lower the fifth a half step, to G♭, to form a C diminished chord (**Example 7c**). For **Example 7d**, revert to the C major triad and raise the fifth a half step, to G♯, to form C augmented.

Going a step further, let's work our way up the neck finding C major chords, using the four highest strings and doubling whichever chord tone is most practical in any given position. In **Example 8**, starting in the open position, as our top note we have

an open E, the third of C major. Then go to the B string and find another chord tone, in this case, C. The open G is the fifth, and if you fret the E on the D string, you'll see a familiar open chord (minus the C you're probably used to playing on the A string). Continue by moving up the fretboard, finding chord tones, while keeping notes in common when possible. Notice how they connect and invert, all forming C major chords, but with the notes stacked in various ways. Call upon your knowledge of the fretboard to stay aware of which notes are which.

Your assignment, one that will be enormously helpful, but will require your full engagement: Take these C major chord forms, or **voicings**, and convert them to minor—remember, just find all the thirds (in this case, E), and lower them a half step to E♭. Come up with comfortable fingerings. Then try to memorize the shapes, but only after you really know which note is which, both in terms of pitch and its role in the triad. Then try both major and minor triads in other keys.

Good luck, and have patience! Your future self with great chord fluency will thank you.

A C chord played in 12th position, on the top four strings.

Increasing Harmony
How to build chords and use them in progression

THE PROBLEM: You've worked to build a solid foundation of music theory, yet need to connect a few more dots in order to feel confident with how the various elements fit together and how to create music with them.

THE SOLUTION: Study the basics of diatonic harmony: understand the theory, then explore on your instrument.

In our previous lessons, you've studied elements of pitch and rhythm, worked on understanding key and time signatures, achieved greater fretboard familiarity, and tackled numerous assignments and exercises that required a significant expenditure of time, patience, and focus. The purpose of this lesson is to draw together the pieces of what we've discussed thus far, apply them as we look at some principles of diatonic harmony, and get you using what you've learned to play and write music. This is another dense lesson, so I recommend a few deep breaths, earplugs if you're someplace noisy, and caffeine or some exercise if you're not fully alert. Once you're ready, have at it!

BUILD MAJOR KEY TRIADS

Western tonal music is fundamentally about tension and release. There are countless ways to navigate between these areas, traversing shades of tension and degrees of resolve through **harmonic progression**—the movement of one chord to another.

As you have seen, every key has an associated scale. Every scale degree has an associated triad. The **tonic**, or chord built on the first scale degree, represents the place of stable musical repose. The **dominant**, built on the fifth degree, is its counterpart—the chord of tension. The **subdominant** chord is built on the fourth degree and often precedes the dominant in harmonic progression. While tonic, subdominant, and dominant chords all have specific meanings (the I, IV, and V, respectively), each chord in a key has a function that falls into one of these categories.

Let's take a look at the chords that result from building a triad on each scale degree. Write out a C major scale, as shown in **Example 1**. We will spell each chord upwards from the root. To review quickly, that means we start with scale degree 1 to find the tonic chord, C. C is the root of the chord. Skip one scale degree to get the third, E. Skip another scale degree for the fifth, G. Remembering what you learned in the previous lesson, look at the intervals to determine the quality of the chord: C to E is a M3, and C to G is a P5, so the tonic chord in the key of C major is—you guessed it—a C major triad. Seems intuitive enough, but now you know why.

The I (C), IV (F), and V (G) chords in the key of C major.

Move to the second scale degree. D is the root. Skip up a scale degree to get the third, F, and another to get the fifth, A. Now analyze the intervals upwards from the root: a m3 and a P5, or a D minor triad. Continue that procedure for all the scale degrees (**Example 2**). The chord quality associated with each scale degree will be the same across all major keys, so it's well worth it to fix them in your mind. With only one exception, all chords within the major mode are major or minor. The chord built on the seventh scale degree—in this case B—is diminished: B to D is a m3, and B to F is a dim5.

REPEAT WITH MINOR KEY CHORDS

Using the same process as in Ex. 2, we'll build the triads of A minor, the relative minor of C major, as shown in **Example 3**. Like in the major mode, the chord qualities you've derived will be the same across all minor keys. As you might have deduced, relative keys share the same notes and therefore the same chords. Context and progression are what allow us to hear them as independent keys.

Often the minor mode will borrow the **leading tone** (seventh scale degree) from the **parallel major mode** (e.g., A minor borrows the note G♯ from A major, as conveyed in **Example 4a**). The leading tone is a very active note, as the half step between it and the tonic creates a strong pull upwards toward resolve. By adopting the leading tone from A major, the dominant chord in the minor mode becomes major and gravitates more strongly toward the tonic—compare the progression with the natural seventh, as in the first measure of **Example 4b**, to that with the raised seventh in the next measure.

FORM SOME MAJOR KEY PROGRESSIONS

Now let's look at some common progressions and transfer them to the fretboard, using just the top four strings. Not only are these voicings useful aesthetically (play them, and hear what I mean), but approaching chords this way will force you to focus on the concepts, rather than falling back on familiar shapes.

Begin by building all the chords in G major (**Example 5**). Then take the ubiquitous I–IV–V–I progression, found across the spectrum of genres: rock, blues, country, folk, soul, indie, classical/baroque, to name just a few. **Example 6a** shows the progression starting in the third position. **Example 6b** moves it up to the fifth position, **Example 6c** to seventh position, and **Example 6d** to tenth position. As you play through these chords, use your harmonic knowledge to identify their notes, find them on the neck, and relate them to the harmony. Don't lean on the tablature, as that defeats the purpose of the exercise and robs you of the experience of putting your efforts into action. Notice how each individual voice moves to the next—take your time so you can really see and hear it. These small movements (also called **voice leading**) make for smoothly connected chord transitions. Next, work through the ii–V–I, one of the most common progressions in jazz and popular music in general, as shown in the key of G in **Examples 7a–7d**.

CLOSE OUT WITH MINOR PROGRESSIONS

Let's move to the key of E minor. First, write out the E minor scale and associated chords (**Example 8**). **Example 9a** shows the i–iv–v–I progression (Em–Am–Bm–Em). As you build these minor chords, notice their close relation to their major counterparts. Find the third(s) in each voicing and move it up a half step, transforming the triad from minor to major. For instance, take the first Em voicing of Ex. 9a, move the Gs on strings 1 and 4 up by one fret each (to G#), and you'll recognize your E major triad.

Example 9b, also in E minor, is identical to Ex. 9a, except that it uses the major V chord (in this case, B). Make your way up the neck, independently discovering the chord voicings in each position for the progression. Finding them for yourself with the knowledge you've been building is hugely beneficial.

Example 10 is yet another progression in E minor, this time using the leading tone of D#, resulting in the harmonies viiº and V. To get that diminished chord better in your brain

and under your fingers, remember that it's just a minor triad with a lowered fifth. You can always start with the more familiar minor chord and move the fifth(s) down by a half step.

For the last set of chords, try another very typical major progression that mixes major and minor diatonic triads: I–vi–ii–V–I, this time in the key of A major. Write out the scale and chords first on your own. You've already worked through ii–V–I movements in Ex. 7, so it's just a matter of adding the vi chord. **Example 11** will get you started, and then you can proceed independently. Once you have these chord progressions down, try them in every key. Work on building the chord forms on the middle four strings and bottom four strings. Then try repeating the process with different chord progressions.

These should not be seen as exercises to go through a few times and then considered checked off an educational to-do list. Spend time with them, and be patient. Try exercises like these for an hour a day for a month, and watch your chord vocabulary, fluency, and neck familiarity skyrocket.

Then write your own progressions. A lot of them. Doing so engages you actively and creatively, etches the concepts more profoundly in your brain, and results in the reward of something that is musically yours. I bet you'll discover many new ideas in the process, and that's the point—when done with the right intention and attitude, study increases inspiration and provides tools for the freer expression of ideas.

An Am chord played in fifth position on the top four strings.

Example 1

Example 4a

Example 4b · **Example 5**

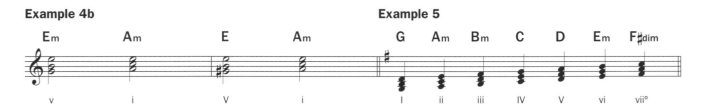

Example 6a · **Example 6b**

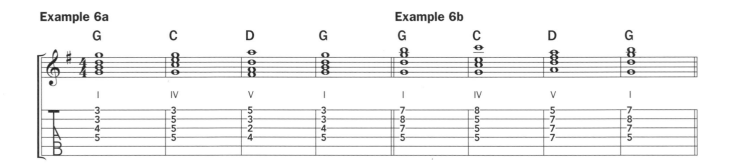

Example 6c · **Example 6d**

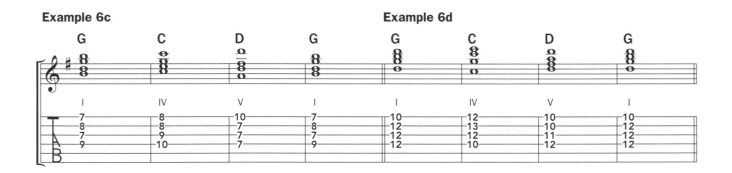

Example 7a · **Example 7b**

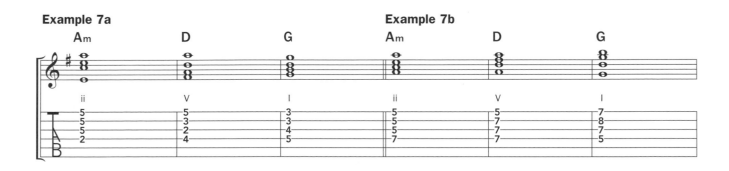

Example 7c   **Example 7d**

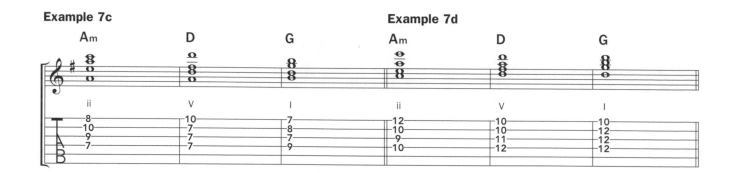

Example 8

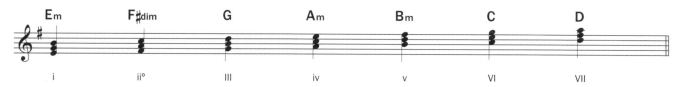

Example 9a   **Example 9b**

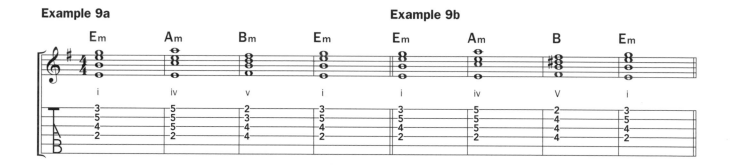

Example 10

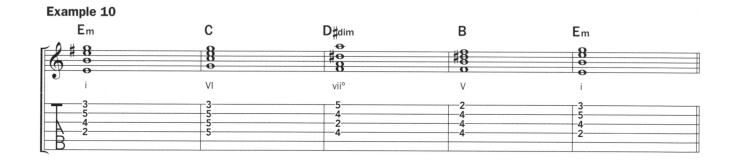

Example 11

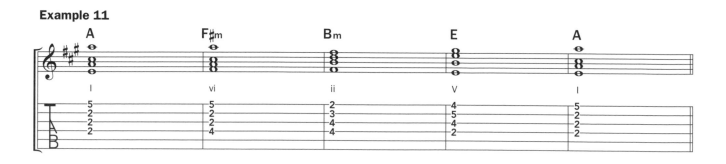

Lucky Sevens

Start enriching your music now with seventh chords

THE PROBLEM: While you're familiar with the basic major and minor triads, any numbers following a chord intimidate you.

THE SOLUTION: Combine your existing knowledge with a little bit of additional theory. Work through a series of exercises to form a foundation for understanding and using seventh chords. Then you won't bat an eye at the harmonies in such songs as Led Zeppelin's version of "Babe I'm Gonna Leave You," Eric Clapton's "Tears in Heaven," or the Beatles' "Yesterday."

The basic concept for seventh chords is simple enough: any number following a chord indicates the note that is to be included in the basic triad to form a more colorful harmony. If you see a 7, this means that in addition to the notes of the triad, you'll also include the note a seventh above the root. The most common seventh chord types are dominant, major, minor, half diminished, and diminished. In this introductory lesson, you'll work with the first three types. Here's how they are constructed:

DOMINANT SEVENTH

If you see a seven following a chord with no further qualification, it's a **dominant seventh chord**—a major triad that includes a minor seventh. It is often simply called a seventh chord and indicated with a 7 following the root name, for example, F7. To build a dominant seventh chord, take any major triad, and add a minor seventh above the root. An easy way to find the minor seventh is to go down a whole step from the root. So if the root is F, a whole step down is E♭, and that F7 chord is spelled F (root), A (major third), C (perfect fifth), E♭ (minor seventh).

An F7 chord played in first position on on strings 1–4.

MAJOR SEVENTH

A **major seventh chord** is a major triad that includes the major seventh. An easy way to find the major seventh is to go down a half step from the root of the chord. If the root is F, a half step down is E. An Fmaj7 chord (also written FM7 or FΔ7) is spelled F (root), A (major third), C (perfect fifth), E (major seventh).

MINOR SEVENTH

To get a **minor seventh chord**, add the minor seventh to a minor triad. An Fm7 chord (also written F-7) contains the notes F (root), A♭ (minor third), C (perfect fifth), and E♭ (minor seventh).

Example 1

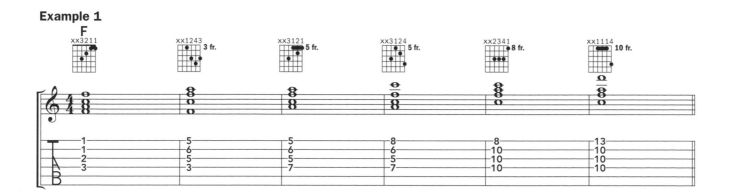

DANIELE GOTTARDO

An Fmaj7 chord played in first position on the top four strings.

TRANSFORM FAMILIAR TRIAD SHAPES INTO DOMINANT SEVENTHS

Start by reviewing major and minor triads. **Example 1** takes you through a review of F major triads in various inversions on the top four strings. **Example 2** does so with F minor triads. Remember, a minor triad can be easily built from its major counterpart by simply moving the third down a half step.

It's also easy to transform major triads into dominant seventh chords. The triads here are all four-note voicings, which means one note in each voicing is doubled. So by moving one of the doubled notes to the seventh, you can create a complete seventh chord. In **Example 3**, start with the familiar F major triad, followed by its associated F7 voicing. This first chord in the series has two Fs, so move the lower of the two—the F on the D string—down a whole step, to E♭.

For the next inversion (**Example 4**), move the higher of the two Fs, falling on the B string, down to E♭. If you're unsure why I told you to choose that F, rather than the lower one, try it the other way, and you'll find it's virtually unplayable unless you have enormous hands or are very high on the neck.

In **Example 5**, the fifth (C) is doubled; move the lower C up to E♭. Then, in both **Example 6** and **Example 7**, move the upper root (F) down to E♭. Note: Not all of these grips are playable on non-cutaway guitars. But learn all the voicings regardless, as when you move to other keys, they will fall at different places on the fretboard, rendering them more or less useful.

REPEAT THE PROCESS, USING MAJOR SEVENTH AND MINOR SEVENTH CHORDS

To create Fmaj7 chords from F triads, you'll do the same thing you did in Examples 3–7. But, as shown in **Example 8**, move one note in each F major chord to E, rather than E♭, to form its major seventh sibling. Similarly, in **Example 9**, you can transform minor triads into minor seventh chords by moving one of the doubled notes in each triad to E♭.

It won't hurt to memorize these chords for use on the fly. But knowing how you built them will help you learn to engineer harmonies all over the neck, and move smoothly between them.

Take it to the next level by playing through the chords in every key. I like making sure I hit them all by moving from one key to the key a fifth below, playing the voicings of, say, E up the neck, then to the nearest voicing of A down the neck, then D up the neck, G down, continuing through C, F, B♭, etc. If you do that for long enough, you'll end up at your starting key, meaning you've navigated around a **circle of fifths**. Try the same exercises using the middle four and bottom four strings. Then make these your seventh chords your own, and write some music with your new vocabulary!

Example 2

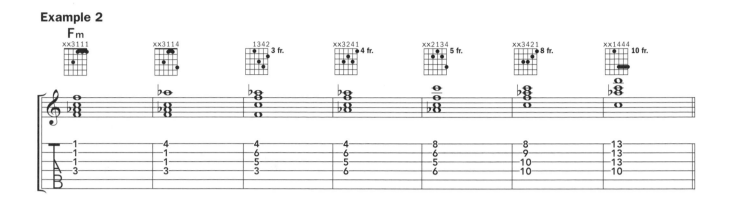

Example 3   **Example 4**   **Example 5**   **Example 6**   **Example 7**

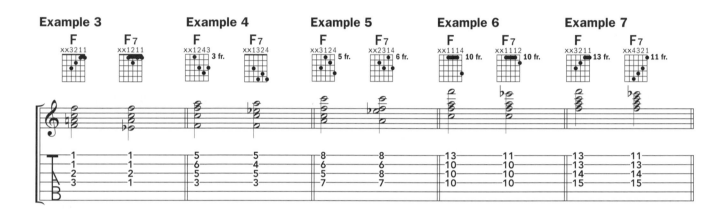

Example 8

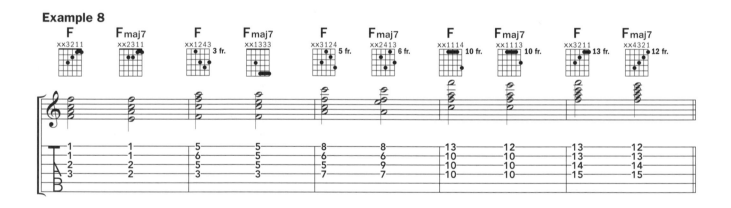

Example 9

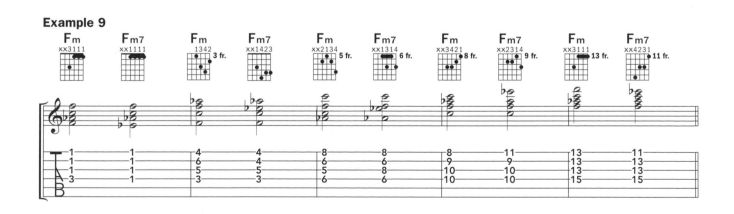

Gimme Five

How to build pentatonic scales up and down the fretboard

THE PROBLEM: You are stuck in one pentatonic scale shape, and anything too far up or down the neck from that familiar shape is uncertain territory.

THE SOLUTION: Use an understanding of theory combined with your fretboard knowledge to conceptualize pentatonic scales, and then map them out across the neck.

The pentatonic scale is everywhere. Its characteristic sound is useful in a wide variety of genres. Yet one particular shape of the pentatonic is far and away the favorite among guitar players. You know the one. You could write an entire course based around classic riffs, lines, and solos derived from the single shape shown in **Figure 1**. This lesson isn't to bash this comfort zone for so many of us, but rather to encourage a little exploration and a more balanced pentatonic vocabulary.

If you've never played a pentatonic scale and have no idea what I'm talking about, fear not. As in all the lessons in this book, you'll build your way up from the essential theory and then apply it to the guitar. The work you've done on major and minor scales will serve you well here.

LEARN THE THEORY

As the name implies, the pentatonic scale is made up of five notes—*penta* (five) *tonic* (tone/note). There are both major and minor pentatonic forms. We have been using the major scale as a point of reference for deriving other scales, and that's again where we will start. Remember, the formula for the major scale is:

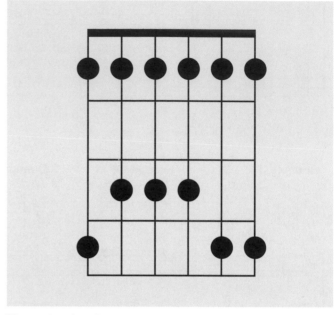

Minor pentatonic scale

or W W H W W W H. To build a **major pentatonic** scale, omit scale degrees 4 and 7: 1 2 3 5 6 (8). To build a **minor pentatonic** scale, leave out scale degrees 2 and 6, and use the minor third and minor seventh (commonly referred to as ♭3 and ♭7). So the construction of the minor pentatonic scale is 1 ♭3 4 5 ♭7 (8).

You may have noticed that deleting these scale degrees also does away with half steps, or minor seconds. The absence of this most tense interval helps give the pentatonic scale its characteristic sound. You're left with whole steps and minor thirds. The formula for the major pentatonic scale is W W m3 W m3 and that for the minor pentatonic is m3 W W m3 W.

Example 1a
C major scale

1 2 3 4 5 6 7 (8)

Example 1b
Delete degrees 4 and 7

1 2 3 ✗ 5 6 ✗ (8)

Example 1c
C major pentatonic scale

1 2 3 5 6 (8)

Example 2
C major pentatonic scale, position VII

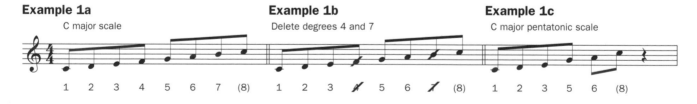

TRANSFER TO THE FRETBOARD

Let's apply all that. Pick a key—start with C major. Write it down somewhere, both the notes and scale degrees, as in **Example 1a**. Delete degrees 4 and 7 (**Example 1b**) to build the C major pentatonic scale (**Example 1c**).

Now look for the scale on the fretboard. Find C on the low E string. Stay in one position and work your way up, finding all the notes of the C major pentatonic until you hit the highest note that is part of the scale on the high E string. The end result should look like what's depicted in **Example 2**. As you play, be mindful both of which note you're playing (E, G, etc.), as well as its relation to C (the third, fifth, etc.). Once you're solidly oriented, you can memorize the scale shape, but don't discard the theory that got you there. You'll also find that the pentatonic scales all fit nicely into two-note-per-string patterns.

MOVE TO THE MINOR

Now try the C minor pentatonic scale using the same steps. As shown in **Example 3a**, first write out the C natural minor scale, then delete the second and sixth degrees (**Example 3b**) to arrive at the minor pentatonic (**Example 3c**). Map out the minor pentatonic on the fretboard—see **Example 4**. Look familiar? It's the go-to minor pentatonic shape. But now you know how it was built, meaning you'll be able to form the other versions of the same scale up and down the neck.

CONSIDER THE RELATIVES

Remember the concept of relative keys—those sharing the same notes but different tonal centers? Every major key has a relative minor, and vice versa. This concept is useful when thinking about pentatonic scales as well. C major and A minor, for instance, are relative keys. **Example 5a** shows the C major pentatonic scale (C D E G A C) next to the A minor pentatonic (A C D E G A) scale, and similarly, **Example 5b** shows G major (G A B D E G) pentatonic and E minor pentatonic (E G A B D E).

Keep in mind that while the two scales share the same notes, they have distinct sounds, as the harmonic context changes the meaning of each. Try playing the notes of C major pentatonic over a static C major chord, and then do the same thing with the same notes over an A minor chord. Hear it?

Your independent mission, should you choose to accept it—and you should!—is to go through the process of constructing and then connecting the major and minor pentatonic scales across the fretboard, just as you did with major and minor scales. You have a head start, as you tackled two of the five scale forms here. It might have occurred to you to just play the major and minor scales you already know, leaving out scale degrees 4 and 7 for the major pentatonic scale and 2 and ♭6 for the minor pentatonic scale. Go right ahead. And you may notice in doing so that the scale also takes on its own form and character. I recommend being able to see the pentatonic scales independently, as well as in relation to the full major and minor scales. The best way to have good orientation is to embrace and overcome disorientation.

Example 3a
C natural minor scale

Example 3b
Delete degrees 2 and ♭6

Example 3c
C minor pentatonic scale

Example 4
C minor pentatonic scale, position VIII

Example 5a
C major pentatonic scale   A minor pentatonic scale

Example 5b
G major pentatonic scale   E minor pentatonic scale

Blues Clues

An introduction to the 12-bar form and its related scale

THE PROBLEM: You've learned the natural minor and minor pentatonic scales, but when you use them in a blues context, they are missing that idiomatic, bluesy sound.

THE SOLUTION: Embark on a study of the blues. Learn the form, the chord changes, the scales, and then start absorbing blues vocabulary by listening to how these elements are used in context.

The blues transcends its own genre. You can find it everywhere. Its characteristic 12-bar form and blue notes permeate jazz, rock, country, soul . . . you name it. Even 20th-century composers such as George Gershwin and Igor Stravinsky incorporated blues elements into their works. The blues is a place where musicians from a wide range of backgrounds and styles can find common ground. It provides a predictable musical backbone, yet allows for countless interpretations, variations, and creative liberties. It's a language with rich and varied dialects—an essential staple of a good vocabulary for any type of musician. In this lesson, we will look at the foundational 12-bar blues.

LEARN THE FORM

The basic 12-bar blues form is shown in **Example 1**. Roman numerals are a common way of expressing key-neutral chord changes—the chords will have the same relation to each other, regardless of the key in which they are played. Minor chords are most often expressed as lowercase Roman numerals, while major chords are expressed with uppercase Roman numerals. The tonic chord in minor—that built on the first scale degree—is indicated as i. Likewise, iv and v are the minor chords built on scale degrees 4 and 5. In a typical blues, the 12-bar progression is repeated throughout.

PLUG IN THE CHORDS

Try the 12-bar form with some chords to get it under your fingers and in your ears. We will start with the guitar-friendly key of E minor. Use your knowledge of scales from previous lessons to spell out the E minor scale, writing scale degrees under each note (**Example 2**).

Then find the i chord. Quick review, but review never hurts: Go to scale degree 1 to get the root of the chord, and the first part of the chord name, E. Now find the other notes of the chord, by skipping one scale degree up from E to get G, the third. Then skip another scale degree to get the fifth, B. It's very common in blues to add a seventh, so skip another scale degree from the fifth to get a D. You have spelled out Em7, the seventh chord built on the first scale degree. Use the same procedure for the iv and v chords, and you'll end up with Am7 (A C E G) and Bm7 (B D F♯ A).

Now go to the fretboard. As you've seen, there are many ways to play seventh chords across the neck. Start with easy voicings shown in **Example 3**. Take a moment to get comfortable with the fingerings, then play through the changes using quarter-note strums (**Example 4**). This sign ✗ means to repeat the previous measure. Once the form is in your ears, try plugging in some moveable voicings that are common in blues, as shown in **Example 5**.

USE THE SCALE

First, play the familiar minor pentatonic over the 12-bar blues form. Enlist a friend, use a backing track, or create a backing

Example 1

i	i	i	i	
iv	iv	i	i	
v	iv	i	v	

Example 2

Example 3

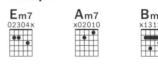

track for yourself using your preferred recording method (playing along to a metronome click and recording with a voice memo app on your smart phone will work). Listen carefully to how each note sounds over each chord. You won't find any strong dissonances using the pentatonic scale—most notes are melodically "safe" to use over all three chords, though you'll notice certain notes (chord tones) are more stable consonances, and non-chord tones introduce tension. There is no release without tension, so experiment with using both, really engaging your ear.

Example 6 shows the E minor **blues scale**. It takes the minor pentatonic scale and adds a *blue note*—the #4 or ♭5— However you name it, it's the note between scale degrees 4 and 5. In the case of E minor, this note is A#/B♭. Try using that blue note over the blues form. Experiment with using it to create tension and resolution. A hint: The note is often resolved by stepwise motion, going either up to the fifth or down to the fourth. Let your ears guide you. If your guitar has access to the higher frets, you can also try the same scale shape at the 12th fret.

Your next assignment is to take the other pentatonic scales you've studied and add the #4/♭5. Then try moving between shapes while playing over the blues changes. Finally, try transposing the moveable chords and scale to different keys. As always, let the resulting shapes—and your memorization of them—be an outgrowth of your understanding. Don't ever check out mentally and lapse into rote finger patterns.

Then do some listening. Listen to B.B. King. Listen to Eric Clapton. Listen to Memphis Minnie, Robert Johnson, Mary Flower, and Derek Trucks. Watch videos of the greats, and absorb the phrasing, the space, the spirit. This lesson is just a place to get some tools and vocabulary to facilitate your journey. But let your heroes and inspirations be your principal guides along the way.

Though you could spend a lifetime becoming fluent in the different dialects of the blues, you'll also benefit from devoting even a modest amount of time to getting familiar with this incredibly varied idiom. Ride that train as long as suits you. Start by studying the basics, and you'll be building a strong foundation for greater nuance and vocabulary. It's well worth it to invest some time in one of the most universal musical languages.

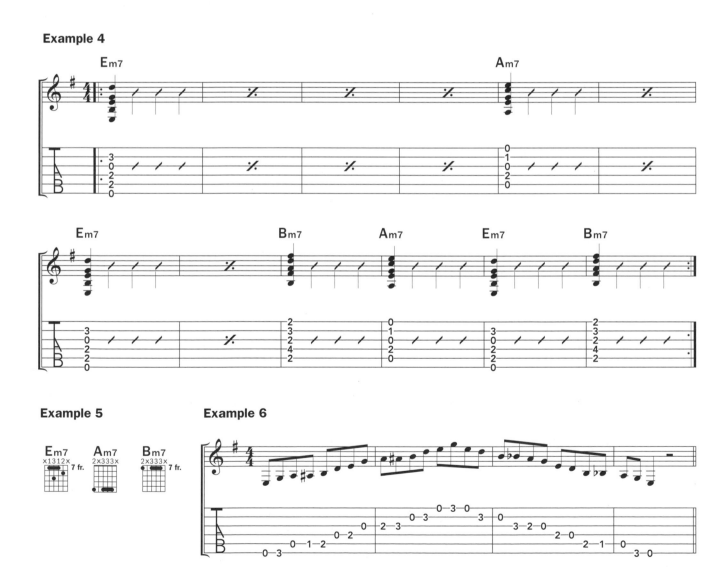

Example 4

Example 5

Example 6

Taking the Lead

Learn to start soloing with these essential building blocks

THE PROBLEM: You're comfortable with chords and holding down rhythms, but when it comes to lead playing or taking a solo, you don't know where to start.

THE SOLUTION: Familiarize yourself with some musical building blocks—scales, arpeggios, and melodic approaches—to write and improvise your own lead lines.

After all the dense lessons, I'm pleased to say much of this one will be review. Here we will focus on putting into practice concepts you've already studied.

Pentatonic scales are an effective and generally manageable way to get started, and many guitar players derive much of their approach from this basic framework.

In the musical examples of this lesson, you'll see another way of notating a scale—pitch notation but with no rhythmic values specified. This kind of notation is common and convenient for outlining scales or any musical ideas where there rhythmic aspect is undefined, not specified, or inconequential.

Example 1a shows the A minor pentatonic scale (A C D E G) starting on the root note of A. Remember, you can also think about this as an A natural minor scale (A B C E F G) that omits the second and sixth scale degrees. Alternatively, these can be viewed as the notes of the C major pentatonic scale—see Ex. 1b. (As we've seen, C major and A minor are relative keys, sharing the same notes). To derive the rela-

Blues guitarists like Memphis Minnie have gotten maximum mileage from pentatonic scales.

tive major from a minor mode, go to the third scale degree. Conversely, the relative minor is found starting on the sixth degree of a major scale.

Examples 2–7 show the sequence of notes starting on each note of the A minor/C major pentatonic scale as it moves up the neck into different positions. To take these raw materials and get started, I recommend two approaches:

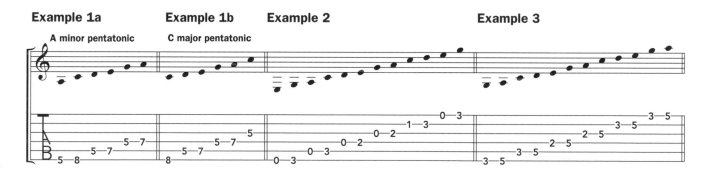

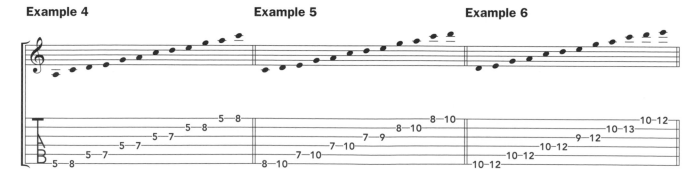

One is necessarily mechanical, the other musical. Now that you've spent ample time working to understand the concepts and derive the scale patterns, I encourage you to go ahead and memorize the shapes. Work to connect them by shifting positions and moving between two positions. Then expand to three, going step-by-step. Don't disconnect from your understanding, but do allow yourself to see and memorize the finger patterns. Get familiar with the scales, their sounds, and how they feel under your fingers. Work on playing them ascending and descending, then try different sequences of notes so that you can skip comfortably between scale degrees.

Next comes the important musical step—creating musical phrases and melodies. I suggest starting out sparingly. Pick one shape and focus on using the notes on only two strings until they become not fingers at the right spot on a fret, but sounds that are musical. Think of short phrases, melodic, or rhythmic motifs. Try bending, slurring, and sliding to notes. Use different note durations. Use vibrato and dynamics. And try to get a limited number of notes to sound expressive.

TRY SOME DIATONIC SCALES

We have already covered major and minor scales. You may have heard of the various modes—Dorian, Phrygian, Mixolydian, and so on. While each of the modes has its characteristic sound and specific applications, I encourage guitarists to start with what is most useful to the type of music you play—in many cases, the major (a.k.a. Ionian) and minor (Aeolian) modes. Of course, you should become versed in all the modes that apply to what you want to do. While we don't have time to cover that here, there are many resources available, included in my suggested reading at the end of this book. In any case, start with a managcable amount of material, learn it well, and then build upon that groundwork that you've created.

Example 8a shows the A minor scale, the relative minor of C major (**Example 8b**). **Examples 9–16** show the sequence of notes starting on the each note of the A minor/C major scale as they move up the neck into different positions. As with the pentatonic scales, work on both the musical and mechanical aspects in smaller sections, then gradually build upon and extend to the entire scale, eventually connecting all the positions.

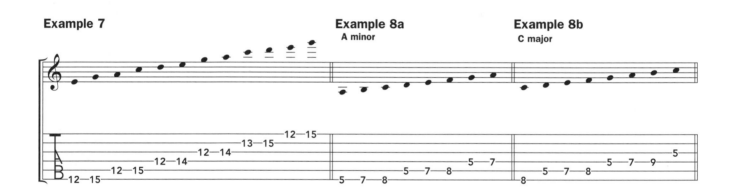

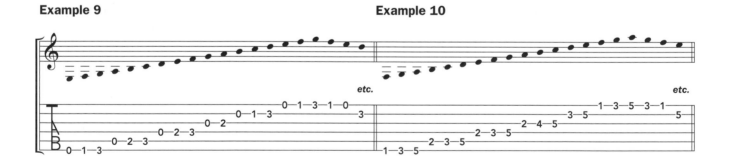

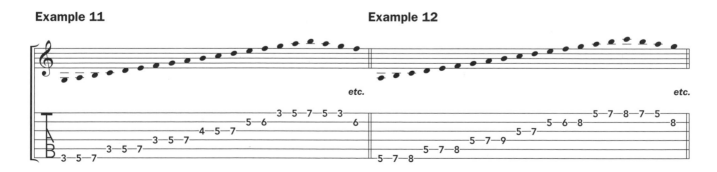

WORK WITH CHORD TONES

An approach that can be quite effective, both melodically and harmonically, is to plan your solos around not just the key of the piece, but the chords over which you're playing. You can use the correct scale and still encounter dissonances as every note relates to the underlying harmony. Take, for example, the A major scale (A B C♯ D E F♯ G♯) over the chords A (A C♯ E) and D (D F♯ A). If you play the fourth degree (D) over the A chord, you'll hear a harsh sound, as the D creates the dissonant interval of a minor second with the chord's C♯. Of course, great improvisers can make any note work, but we are focusing on the basics here.

ARPEGGIOS

Arpeggios are chords played melodically (sequentially) rather than harmonically (simultaneously). To start studying them, take some of the triads and seventh chords you've already learned, and work on playing them one note at a time. The tendency may initially be to hold down the full chord and pick through individual notes. That's fine and has various applications, but also try moving from note to note like a melodic line, picking up each finger as you move to the next note so you hear only only note at a time. This is helpful for gaining more familiarity and a new perspective on chords, as well as greater finger dexterity and independence. But most importantly, arpeggios are very effective melodic building blocks which can be your ticket out of the tendency to overuse stepwise motion (moving from one scale degree to the next adjacent note).

Example 17 shows an A major arpeggio followed by a D major arpeggio to outline a I–IV progression. **Example 18** moves toward a more musical approach while sticking mostly to the chord tones and incorporating only a few non-chord tones. These **passing tones** are of shorter duration and placed on weaker beats, which gives them more of a connecting and color function—the ear hears them as a step along the path to the goal, which is a chord tone.

PLAY THEMES AND VARIATIONS

With a foundation of some scales and arpeggios, you can create comprehensible lines. One effective way to do so is to take a clear, concise theme—it can be melodic, rhythmic, or both—

Being able to hear a melody before you play it will expand your musicality.

PRISCILLA DU PREEZ

and make variations to develop it. Start with a skeletal motif, like in **Example 19** (which happens to be identical to the first measure of Ex. 18). You can add notes to embellish it, as in **Examples 20a–20c**. You can change the rhythms, as in **Examples 21a–21c**. You can fragment it, as in **Examples 22a–22c**, where an ever-smaller section of the motif is compressed and repeated.

HEAR, SING, PLAY

Something to work on, both as an immediate and long-term goal, is creating melodies in your mind before applying them to the fretboard. Listen to the music over which you'll be soloing and try hearing a melody in your mind, even if it's simple, obvious, or uninspired at first. The idea is to start encouraging your mind to invent melodies. Sing the melody. Make it memorable—so memorable that you can find it on the guitar and sing with your fingers.

Here we are cracking open an enormous subject. Don't let the scope deter you. The path of improvisation and composition is endless, and that's part of its beauty.

There is always more to learn. Start at the beginning, gather your tools along the way, and forge the path that is right for you.

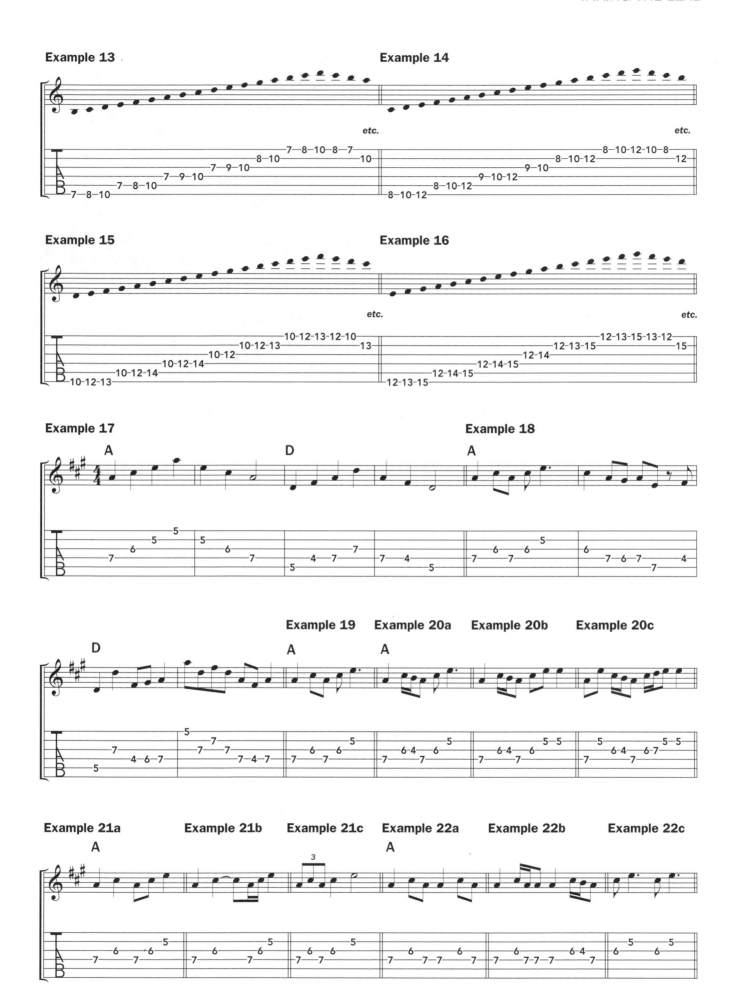

ESSENTIAL READING

As I send you off on the next phase of your journey, I want to give you my recommendations for what I consider essential reading material. —*GM*

Tonal Harmony, Stefan Kostka, Dorothy Payne, Byron Almen
My go-to reference for clear, concise, comprehensive harmony and theory.

Zen Guitar, Philip Toshio Sudo
You'll find no theoretical or guitar-specific exercises, but rather a wealth of wisdom to prime your attitude and approach along the lifelong path of music.

Peak: Secrets from the New Science of Expertise, Anders Ericsson and Robert Pool
Well-researched, with solid scientific data, this book convincingly dispels many myths and unhelpful notions about talent and expertise.

The Obstacle Is the Way, Ryan Holiday
Based in Stoic philosophy, this provides wisdom on how we perceive and confront challenges.

BILL EVANS

ABOUT THE AUTHOR

Gretchen Menn is a guitarist and composer based in the San Francisco Bay Area. She writes, records, and performs original music, and is the guitarist of the popular Led Zeppelin tribute band Zepparella. Menn plays a Stephen Strahm Eros steel-string.
gretchenmenn.com

More Tools to Get You Started

Let the bestselling *Acoustic Guitar Method* by David Hamburger be your guide to the joys of playing the guitar.

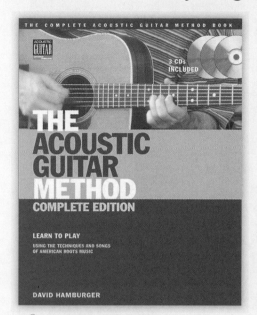

The COMPLETE Acoustic Guitar Method

The *Acoustic Guitar Method* is the only beginning guitar method based on traditional American music that teaches you authentic techniques and songs. From the folk and blues music of yesterday have come the rock, country, and jazz of today. Understand, play, and enjoy these essential traditions and styles on the instrument that truly represents American music, the acoustic guitar. This comprehensive approach is the one tool you need to get started. **$24.95**, 136 pp., 9" x 12", HL00695667

Acoustic Guitar Method, Book One

LESSONS First Chords, First Song | New Chord, New Strum | Tab Basics and Your First Melody | Reading Notes | The G Chord | The C Chord | More Single Notes | Country Backup Basics | Seventh Chords | Waltz Time | Half Notes and Rests | Minor Chords | A Minor-Key Melody | The B7 Chord.
SONGS Columbus Stockade Blues | Careless Love | Darling Corey | East Virginia Blues | In the Pines | Banks of the Ohio | Scarborough Fair | Shady Grove | Man of Constant Sorrow | and more!
$9.95, 48 pp., 9" x 12", HL00695648

Acoustic Guitar Method, Book Two

LESSONS The Alternating Bass | Blues in E | Major Scales and Melodies | Starting to Fingerpick | More Picking Patterns | The G-Major Scale | Bass Runs | More Bass Runs | Blues Basics | Alternating-Bass Fingerpicking | Fingerpicking in 3/4.
SONGS Columbus Stockade Blues | Stagolee | The Girl I Left Behind Me | Shady Grove | Shenandoah | Will the Circle Be Unbroken? | Sail Away Ladies | I Am a Pilgrim | Bury Me Beneath the Willow | Alberta | Sugar Babe | House of the Rising Sun.
$9.95, 48 pp., 9" x 12", HL00695649

Acoustic Guitar Method, Book Three

LESSONS The Swing Feel | Tackling the F Chord | More Chord Moves | Introducing Travis Picking | Travis Picking, Continued | Hammer-ons, Slides, and Pull-offs | Alternate Bass Notes | The Pinch | All Together Now.
SONGS Frankie and Johnny | Delia | Gambler's Blues | Banks of the Ohio | Crawdad | New River Train | Sail Away Ladies | Little Sadie | Omie Wise | That'll Never Happen No More.
$9.95, 48 pp., 9" x 12", HL00695666

Dive Deeper into Chords, Slide, and Jazz

Learn authentic techniques and expand your understanding of musical essentials

The Acoustic Guitar Method Chord Book

David Hamburger's supplementary chord book for the *Acoustic Guitar Method* is a must-have resource for building your chord vocabulary! Start with a user-friendly explanation of what chords are and how they are named, then learn chords by key in all 12 keys, with both open-position and closed-position voicings for each common chord type.
$5.95, 48 pp., 9" x 12", HL00695722

Acoustic Guitar Slide Basics

Bitten by the blues bug? Want to explore the haunting sounds of acoustic slide guitar or brush up on your bottleneck basics? This easy-to-follow, step-by-step book and CD will help you master one of the great styles of American roots music. LESSONS | Single-String Melodies | Working in the Thumb | Moving Around the Neck | Spicing Up Your Melodies | Travis Picking | and more!
$16.95, 72 pp., 9" x 12", HL00695610

Early Jazz and Swing Songs for Guitar

Add early jazz and swing standards to your repertoire! Learn full guitar parts, read detailed notes on the song origins, and hear a two-guitar recording of each tune. SONGS After You've Gone | Avalon | Baby, Won't You Please Come Home | Ballin' the Jack | Hindustan | Limehouse Blues | Rose Room | Saint James Infirmary | St. Louis Blues | Whispering | and more! **$9.95**, 40 pp., 9" x 12", HL00695867

Buy online at
store.AcousticGuitar.com

THE WAY MUSIC WORKS

 Shop **store.AcousticGuitar.com** for books, guides, and more from *Acoustic Guitar*.

Get to know the music, musicians, and instruments that matter. For beginning to professional guitarists, teachers, and members of the trade, too.

Information, instruction, and inspiration for every guitar player. Reference, how-to, songbooks, and more.

From lessons and songs to tuners and tees, the Acoustic Guitar store has something for you. Visit **store.acousticguitar.com** today.

The Acoustic Guitar website features stories you won't want to miss—gear reviews, breaking news, performance videos, giveaways, lessons, and more. Visit **AcousticGuitar.com**.